NO LONGER PROPERTY
OF ANY
RANGEVIEW LIBRARY
DISTRICT

Advance Praise for *The Fundable Startup: How Disruptive Companies Attract Capital*

"Every entrepreneur can benefit from the thoughtful advice in *The Fundable Startup*. The book offers a proven framework for evaluating product ideas, attracting management talent, and raising capital for a new venture. The anecdotal stories are entertaining and show firsthand how others have successfully built their businesses around the fundamental principles in Dr. Haney's book. *The Fundable Startup* is a must-read for company founders!"

—John W. Jarve
Managing Director, Menlo Ventures

"*The Fundable Startup* is a bible of information; a must-read for entrepreneurs! It lights the road for successful venturing activity."

—Robert Gottdener
Director, Wayne Brown Institute

"In *The Fundable Startup*, Dr. Fred Haney provides a realistic and multifaceted view into the skill sets and resources required to build a successful tech startup. Highly experienced on both sides of the table—as both a startup CEO and an investor—Dr. Haney is uniquely qualified to advise the next generation of tech entrepreneurs as they embark on their journey. Insightful and inspiring, *The Fundable Startup* provides invaluable guidance on how to build your entrepreneurial leadership team and attract the resources that will make your startup a success."

—Dr. Helena Yli-Renko
Director, Lloyd Greif Center for Entrepreneurial Studies
Marshall School of Business, University of Southern California

"Innovators vs. Accelerators—Founders and Seasoned CEOs. Fred delivers excellent advice and actionable steps every executive can leverage daily to attract capital and be a money magnet CEO. Our company LiveSafe greatly benefited in our early days from Fred's experience and this book shares his wisdom on attracting investors and talent for your startup."

—Carolyn Parent
President and CEO of LiveSafe

"Fred Haney's book, *The Fundable Startup*, is filled with practical information on starting a company and positioning it for funding. I wish it had been around when I formed my first company. While Fred's mechanical advice is flawless, my favorite chapter was 'The Solution: Be a Money Magnet.' Once you have a reputation for growing a successful company you find the VCs call you. Fred helps the first-time entrepreneur understand how to get to that place where the law of attraction has a chance to work. That's valuable!"

—Walter Cruttenden
Founder-Chairman, Acorns

"In *The Fundable Startup*, Dr. Haney provides practical insights in deceptively simply language to the key questions on every entrepreneur's mind. The developing executive will appreciate Fred's triangulation of success factors through both case studies and summarized lessons drawn from his unique depth of experience."

—Shawn Abbott
iNovia Capital

"Few entrepreneurs building high potential companies know how to make their startups appealing to investors. Drawing on his experience on both sides of the table, Fred Haney has produced a masterful guide to creating fundable startups. If you want to improve your odds of raising money, read this book before you launch an equity crowdfunding campaign or talk to angel investors or venture capitalists."

—Scott Shane
Professional angel investor
Case Western Reserve University entrepreneurship professor

"*The Fundable Startup* is much more than a conventional book about venture capital and entrepreneurial vigor. It speaks in practical terms—no jargon, no clichés—about raising capital and attracting the skills needed to build a business and finding a manager to run a growing concern. The book asks the right questions on many fronts, such as:

> How would you forecast revenues and expenses—because if you get that one wrong, where is the profit?
> How would you judge a technology transfer from university research to pluck out a product that will benefit users and find customers?
> Why might executives from large companies not be the ideal choice to run small companies?
> Importantly, this book speaks to the job of choosing a manager, a different discipline from entrepreneurship. Management is a process of long-term learning that enables people and organizations to grow into successful institutions.

The Fundable Startup brushes aside clichés, such as 'I invest in people . . .' Instead . . . One invests in ideas and people. Entrepreneurial companies are exciting, but keep in mind that 'activity is not achievement.'

Author Fred Haney has founded high-tech companies, and helped a score more such companies as director. He has managed divisions of large companies, founded venture capital networks, and managed successful investment in eighty startup companies."

—James Flanigan
Business columnist and author
54 years of business journalism, including *Forbes* for 18 years,
assistant managing editor *Los Angeles Times* for 22 years

"*The Fundable Startup* is the perfect book for a first-time CEO of a startup. After personally working with Dr. Haney during the early stages of Parcel Pending, I found him and *The Fundable Startup* to be invaluable. With so much unknown for a first-time CEO, *The Fundable Startup* demonstrates many of the critical issues and needs that every CEO must learn. Dr. Haney is the ideal author as he has such deep experience with startups and organizations at every level. *The Fundable Startup* is a must-read for all entrepreneurs and first time CEOs."

—Lori A. Torres
CEO, Parcel Pending Inc.

"Fred Haney has provided an inspired road map for startup companies to build extraordinary value for their ultimate acquisition or IPO.

Having served for 44 years as the chairman of Cappello Global LLC, a global boutique investment bank whose principals have transacted over $100 billion in business spanning 55 countries, and having served as a director of dozens of public and private companies, I have first-hand knowledge of thousands of businesses, and I am very aware of how value is created, measured, and monetized.

Fred's focus on value-creating milestones and building strong management teams is key to a successful startup as well as any growing business.

Fred is living proof of one of his fundamental premises: that experience matters. Having personally served with Fred on the board of directors of Caldera Medical Inc. for over five years and experienced Fred's laser focus on the creation of value and strong teams, he is the real deal! His leadership and sage wisdom has had a profound impact on the company.

When almost any issue arises, Fred has dealt with a similar situation in the past. He is living proof that experience does in fact matter. His knowledge is almost encyclopedic, practical, and well-articulated.

Many of Fred's messages apply to more mature companies as well as startups. Most of the companies we work with are well beyond the startup stage but they would do well to follow Fred's advice. For example, many mature companies should increase their focus on creating value and making sure they have the right team of people in place.

Everyone—both the experienced and the inexperienced—will enjoy and benefit from reading *The Fundable Startup*."

—Alexander L. Cappello
Chairman and CEO of Cappello Global, LLC
Past Chairman of YPO International (Young Presidents Organization)

"I started my first two ventures while I was an undergraduate at Caltech. They failed.

Only after a career that included chapters as a research scientist and engineer; corporate executive; turn-around specialist; CEO, chairman, and director of a number of public and closely-held companies; university professor; and consultant to companies and government agencies around the globe, did I have the knowledge and experience to become a successful serial entrepreneur.

Most would-be entrepreneurs, lacking depth of experience, fail in their first ventures, while developing a history that makes it extraordinarily challenging to secure the funds necessary to make another try.

Fred Haney has consolidated in his book, *The Fundable Startup*, a body of learning to arm entrepreneurs with the knowledge necessary to anticipate and address problems and capitalize on opportunities. Well dog-eared copies should be on the desks of every would-be entrepreneur and their team members and advisers."

—Michael M. Mann, PhD
Chairman and CEO, Blue Marble Companies
Executive Chairman, Creso Global, Inc.
Executive Chairman, SprintRay, Inc.
Chairman, Transient Plasma Systems, Inc.

"*The Fundable Startup* is a book that needed to be written and should be read by anyone contemplating a startup venture or hoping to advise entrepreneurial activities. It addresses in easy-to-read fashion the now obsolete concept that a novel idea alone is worth a $1 million plus venture funding valuation. Notwithstanding the opinion of many that founders are the best leaders of emerging companies, my experience has been that the predominant reason for the failure of a startup is an inexperienced leader who doesn't know what he or she doesn't know. This book provides the criteria for a founder to determine whether he or she is the appropriate person to lead the company and a roadmap to successfully attracting investment capital.

I've had the opportunity to work with Dr. Haney from time to time, both for the same and opposing parties, and am always impressed with his understanding of the issues and his professional approach to solutions. In *The Fundable Startup*, Dr. Haney not only demonstrates the educational and professional background to write a tutorial on startup ventures, he has provided a wealth of background information for the aspiring founder."

—Richard Hansen
Partner in the law firm of Hansen Seto, LLP,
specializing in matters related to startups, emerging companies, corporate/
business transactions, exit strategies (mergers, acquisitions)
and intellectual property licensing

"Ronald Reagan's 'Trust by verify' quote has always resonated with me. Meaning we hear, see, and read a tremendous amount of data and opinions, but which are backed up with proven content? Many books have been written about how to fund your startup, mostly by individuals who have been successful in at least one funding. But therein lies the challenge!

Funding a startup is not linear or singular. It is a very complex game with multiple players with different goals, on different playing fields, all trying to score at the same time. For that reason and my 'Trust by verify' mentality I found Fred Haney's new book *The Fundable Startup* to be extraordinary. Fred provides data, examples, and amazing analogies that support his sage advice to startup CEOs.

The Fundable Startup provides startup founders and CEOs with options— creative and proven successful options. In fact, I have never read a funding manual/textbook that comes anywhere close to providing the number of real-world tactical approaches to raising funds as *The Fundable Startup*."

—Michael Sawitz
CEO, FastStart.studio, a mixed-use business incubator

"I wish Fred's book *The Fundable Startup* had been available during the two startups in which I was involved. Not only does Fred give the aspiring entrepreneur a roadmap to successfully fund her venture, he provides needed context and relevant information on the different types of funding sources— how they think and what they are looking for when reviewing and analyzing opportunities. Reading this book is like having someone alongside you who has 'been there and done that' and mentors you along the way. You'll learn the pitfalls to avoid, the pros and cons of different growth and funding strategies, and what investors value most in making their decisions. It's truly a must-read for the entrepreneur seeking outside funding."

—Barri Carian
Principal, Carian Consulting

"*The Fundable Startup* is a MUST-read for entrepreneurs seeking funding. It makes a confusing process seem simple and straightforward.

Fred Haney has distilled fundraising for startups to a very understandable sequence of logical events that can greatly improve a company's chances of raising capital.

Fred's unique perspective garnered from having been a corporate planner, venture capital manager, angel investor, and cofounder provides enormous insight.

This book could easily be named 'The Truth About Startups' or 'Startup Tales of Truth.' Every entrepreneur should read it to save heartaches and get a clear picture of what works!

Concepts of value, capital, talent and execution are inextricably woven together in realistic examples and case studies. Fred connects to the reality of the process helping entrepreneurs set realistic expectations for the funding of their dreams."

—Don Lavoie, PhD
President and CEO, Developmetrics

"The most frequently asked question of an educator of entrepreneurship is 'Are entrepreneurs born or made?' Some hold strongly to the former, yet over the past fifteen years, I have learned that a successful entrepreneur must build a mind-set, skill set, and tool set. *The Fundable Startup* is an outstanding road map to build all three sets."

—Patrick Henry
Assistant Professor, Clinical Entrepreneurship Director,
University Venturing Summit,
Llyod Greif Center for Entreprneurial Studies
USC/Marshall School of Business

"Fred Haney's experience as an executive, global venture capitalist, and angel investor provides invaluable insights as to how companies attract capital. This is a must-read for all entrepreneurs positioning their idea and company for success! *The Fundable Startup* answers the chicken and the egg questions that startups face: 'how to attract both capital and top executive talent.' I highly recommend it to all founders."

—Mark J. Landay
Dynamic Synergy Executive Recruitment
Chairman Emeritus, HBS Angels of Southern California

"*The Fundable Startup* is a well-written book and provides insight for those with the entrepreneurial spirit to move onward and upwards with their dreams and passions. The author is essentially a 'harbor pilot' to help people navigate successfully through the pitfalls of starting and managing a disruptive company that can attract capital. For high-tech startups, passion and commitment are necessary ingredients for the founders. However, getting funding/cash for a high-tech startup depends on the founder being able to find a capable fundable management team with an experienced CEO who knows how to attract cash. As stated at the end of Chapter 3, 'Learning from the 99%,' sound, capable leadership is the key to success.

The thirteen chapters end with the last chapter entitled 'Follow the Leader.' The last sentence of this final chapter ends fabulously with a quote from the famous football player, coach, and executive Vince Lombardi: 'Contrary to the opinions of many, leaders are not born; they are made. And they are made by hard effort, which is the price that we must all pay for success' from his book *What It Takes to Be #1*.

For many years at the monthly Monday Club meetings in Orange County, CA, which he chairs, Fred Haney has provided thoughtful questions for each presenter of a startup company. His perception of what is required for these companies is more than intuitive and is due to his vast knowledge of what a startup company requires in order to move forward. After forty years of experience, Fred Haney writes clearly and logically about entrepreneurship and leadership. The book is easy to read, logical, and it has great insight for business school students, founders, and inexperienced CEOs."

"I have learned to use the word *impossible* with the greatest caution."
—WERNHER VON BRAUN, rocket engineer, father of rocket technology
and space science in the United States, NASA engineering program manager,
chief architect of the Saturn V launch vehicle that propelled the Apollo
manned lunar missions to the moon.

—Corinne G. Wong, PhD
CEO, SCLERA, LLC

"As chairman and initial investor in Media Matchmaker, a disruptive media ad technology company, Fred Haney taught us the ABC's of successful entrepreneurship. *The Fundable Startup* breaks down his basic philosophies and techniques into short, easily understandable chapters. A must-read for anyone considering diving into the *real* 'Shark Tank.'"

—Jim Mahoney
President, Media Matchmaker

"Fred Haney's decades of experience as an entrepreneur and investor translate to invaluable and practical guidance to those seeking capital to start and scale dynamic ventures. Business is about improving the odds, and *The Fundable Startup* does that."

—David Belasco
Executive Director and Professor
Greif Center for Entrepreneurial Studies
USC Marshall School of Business

The
Fundable
Startup

The
Fundable
Startup

★

How Disruptive Companies
Attract Capital

Fred M. Haney, PhD

SelectBooks, Inc.
New York

Copyright © 2018 by Fred M. Haney, PhD

All rights reserved. Published in the United States of America. No part of this book may be reproduced or transmitted in any form or by any means, graphic, electronic, or mechanical, including photocopying, recording, taping or by any information storage or retrieval system, without the permission in writing from the publisher.

This edition published by SelectBooks, Inc.
For information address SelectBooks, Inc., New York, New York.

First Edition

ISBN 978-1-59079-432-6

Library of Congress Cataloging-in-Publication Data

Names: Haney, Fred M., author.
Title: The fundable startup : how disruptive companies attract capital /
Fred
  M. Haney, PhD.
Description: First Edition. | New York : SelectBooks, Inc., [2018] |
Includes
  bibliographical references and index.
Identifiers: LCCN 2017006696 | ISBN 9781590794326 (pbk. : alk. paper)
Subjects: LCSH: New business enterprises. | Information
  technology--Management. | Strategic planning.
Classification: LCC HD62.5 .H3635 2018 | DDC 658.1/1--dc23 LC record
available at https://lccn.loc.gov/2017006696

Book design by Janice Benight

Manufactured in the United States of America
10 9 8 7 6 5 4 3 2 1

*To my loving and understanding wife
of fifty-three years, Barbara, who has patiently
and supportingly shared every success and every failure,
and who helped tremendously with the conception
and editing of this book.*

Contents

Foreword

By John E. Edwards, Jr., MD, Distinguished Emeritus Professor of Medicine, David Geffen School of Medicine at UCLA and Senior Investigator, LA Biomedical Research Institute at Harbor/UCLA Medical Center.

The Los Angeles Biomedical Research Institute at Harbor/UCLA Medical Center (LABomed) is an independent medical research facility, which was established to manage research led by faculty members of the David Geffen School of Medicine at UCLA who are based at the medical school affiliate LA County hospital. I am one of those faculty members and was the Chief of the Infectious Diseases Division of the Harbor/UCLA hospital for over three decades. After approximately thirty-five years of laboratory research, with five colleagues, we were encouraged by the FDA to take our vaccine for Candida infections into clinical trials.

Candida is a fungus which lives normally on the body, but can become lethal in patients who have been exposed to a variety of modern medical therapeutics. Unfortunately, a patient who has been treated with medical advances such as powerful, broad spectrum antibiotics, implantation of nonhuman materials, including intravenous catheters, and immunosuppression for treatment of cancer and preservation of transplanted organs, is more likely to become infected. Infection with this organism has become very common.

All our work on this vaccine had been funded mainly by the National Institutes of Health (NIH). The amount of funding needed to enter clinical trials was beyond the scope of NIH funding, and we were encouraged to form a company to enable human trials. Fred Haney had been on the Foundation Board of LABiomed. The CEO of the research institute asked Fred, who had a wealth of experience in venture capital startups, to help us. None of us had any experience in starting a company, and Fred's volunteering to help was critically important. Fred had over forty years of experience in venture capital and company startups. Had it not been for Fred's help, I doubt that we would ever started our company, called NovaDigm Therapeutics, and would never have performed any clinical trials.

Once Fred began meeting with us, it became evident that his years of experience had provided him with an abundance of knowledge about the process of startup, down to virtually every detail and concept. Additionally, he had numerous critically important personal contacts in business law, business schools, venture capitalists, angel investors, accountants, business consultants, patent strategy experts, and business bankers. It was also clear that he had extensive experience and depth of understanding of the principles of entrepreneurship, leadership, and personnel management in the context of teamwork.

Discovering the breadth of Fred's experience in startups alleviated concerns we had regarding our own lack of experience in the startup space. In chapter 1 of this book, Fred addresses how founders frequently under-estimate the magnitude of the task necessary to successfully start a company. When we began to form NovaDigm, we had the additional problem of not having the time necessary for the task. All of us, as part of our academic affiliation, had responsibilities beyond research in the area of teaching, and some of us had patient care responsibilities. Fortunately, we recognized these time and experience limitations, and were extremely grateful for the time Fred put into our startup effort.

Throughout this book, Fred discusses qualities needed in the CEO of a successful startup company. Of great importance, in chapter 3, he discusses in detail the issue of obtaining an experienced CEO when a startup has little or no funding and he suggests strategies for solutions. This is a complex issue and is critical to solve. Both his discussion of solutions to this issue and Fred's direct assistance were invaluable to us. In chapters 9 and 10, Fred discusses in detail the desirable qualities of a CEO, and their critical importance to the success of the startup.

In our specific circumstance, we had a complex problem to solve in addition to finding the right CEO. There has never been a fungal vaccine approved by the FDA for humans and this was only the second time a fungal vaccine had ever been tested in humans in a placebo controlled trial. Since our vaccine was intended to be used in hospitalized patients who had very serious healthcare-associated infections, a trial in that population was going to be very expensive, costing many millions of dollars. It was going to be nearly impossible to obtain that level of funding without a proof of principle showing the feasibility of protecting humans with a fungal vaccine. Therefore, it was necessary to devise a clinical trial for a disease that would not put patients receiving a placebo at risk for any serious, life threatening consequences. We chose to test the vaccine first in patients who had mucosal candidiasis, rather than infection in the deep, vital organs, such as the brain, heart, and kidneys. If the vaccine ultimately showed effect in these deep organ infections, it would have value orders of magnitude beyond the mucosal infections. Yet protection of the mucosa would be of value by itself. The challenge was to create a clear picture of the ultimate value of the vaccine and the company.

In chapter 4, Fred discusses, in detail, strategies to create and build such value in the startup company.

In efforts to convert an important medical treatment into an entity that can make a major impact on the growing problem of lethal healthcare-associated infections in hospitalized patients, I have learned, beyond measure, the intricacies of technical transfer through the startup process. Fred Haney has been absolutely essential to our gaining the resources, forming NovaDigm Therapeutics, and completing the first trial in humans of a fungal vaccine showing a signal of efficacy. Fred's book covers every circumstance we encountered at the beginning and continue to face as we move forward.

The book is written in a logical and linear style, with frequently entertaining and valuable anecdotes and case studies from his many startup successes over more than four decades. Additionally, he has woven the strategies into changes and trends of the business community, and national and international economic. The principles he discusses apply not only to biomedical startups, but to the process in general, regardless of the "product." I will certainly be encouraging any colleagues I know who are starting to bring their technology into the private sector to read this extremely thoughtful and valuable commentary. I just wish I had access to the book before we embarked on this complex technical transfer project, but then, we did have access to Fred!

Preface

Living in a world of problems and solutions, I am constantly asking eager entrepreneurs, "What problem are you solving?" For this reason, it would be fair to ask, "What problem is this book solving?"

In my opinion, too many startup companies fail unnecessarily. Is this a broadly recognized problem? I suspect not. The people involved in the startup company industry are gainfully employed and may not be aware of this high failure rate. Did the horse and buggy people think they had a problem? Probably not until the automobile was invented. This may be a similar situation. It may not look like a problem until people realize that there is a far better way to build startup companies.

Why do I think there is a problem here? Small Business Administration statistics show that, in recent years, company failures have outnumbered company survivors.* Because of my mentoring network, Monday Club, and my involvement with companies at very early stages, I see a different issue: Many companies fail before they become a statistic. Many companies fail before they even get incorporated.

I have followed my prescribed model for startups for over thirty years, but I could not have always articulated it clearly. My first recognition that there is a problem came to me as a realization that some aspects of the startup company process do not work well. I observed, for example, that many incubator approaches do

---

*SBA Office of Advocacy, "Frequently Asked Questions about Small Business," September, 2012, accessed January 2, 2017, www.sba.gov/advocacy.

not work because the founder being "incubated" simply does not have enough skills to build a successful company. It took a few years for me to articulate the model I had followed for years: "Create value and attract capital. Don't just start pleading with investors for money." Overall, this book is the product of fifty years of experience and about four years of concentrated effort to clarify the message.

Does every startup company deserve to succeed? Of course, not. It takes a truly big idea, or a solution to a very important problem, to justify creating a new company. But I see too many companies with good ideas that never get their invention to market. The failure is usually traceable to a founder who simply "doesn't know what he, or she, doesn't know."

I am not saying that an inexperienced founder cannot succeed in building a company. There will be more founders like Steve Jobs and Bill Gates. My message is that the odds greatly favor the leader and management team who have experience and a track record of success.

If you are a startup company founder, do not read this book to find out how to become a successful CEO. Read it to find out how to attract the people who can help make your company successful. Follow Parcel Pending founder Lori Torres's mantra, "I can solve any problem. I just need to find the people who can help me solve it."

The Fundable Startup presents a tested approach to creating a startup company. The essence is for the startup company to create as much value as possible before approaching investors. This allows companies to attract capital, rather than begging for it. The book contains a number of examples of founders that followed this approach successfully.

The lessons of this book are described in ten case studies based on my personal interviews with the participants. I am very grateful to Dr. Jack Edwards, Steve Casselman, Lori Torres, Josh Roach, Shy Pahlevani, and Bryon Merade for sharing their startup stories.

Thanks also to Jeremy Wall for sharing his insights about incubators and accelerators.

I am also very grateful to Dr. Webb Castor, former VP Xerox Corporation, and Van Honeycutt, former CEO and Chairman of Computer Sciences Corporation, for sharing their journeys from the bottom rung of the corporate ladder to the top rung. The top CEOs build their success on extensive experience and a long list of skills. This is a lesson that should not go unheeded by the ambitious entrepreneur.

Thanks, also, to my friends Alex Cappello, Bob Gottdener, Dr. Gregory Mason, Mark Landay, Lori Torres, Steve Casselman, Preston Landon, Dr. Webb Castor, Van Honeycutt, and Shy Pahlevani for providing extensive and helpful feedback on the manuscript.

I am doubly grateful to Dr. Jack Edwards for providing feedback on an early draft and for writing an insightful and gracious foreword.

My associates in Venture Management have been extremely helpful in the evolution of this book. Barbra Ongwico provided early inspiration. Amy (Hvitfeldtsen) Zytkiewicz helped shape the ideas in the very early stages. Mike Will Downey provided insightful editing, helpful marketing assistance, and skilled website development.

Thanks, as well, to Bill Gladstone, of Waterside Productions, for connecting me with SelectBooks, and thanks to Minda Wilson for introducing me to Bill. Terry Somerson, my editor, made extensive and helpful comments on the manuscript. And, finally, thanks to Nancy Sugihara, Kenzi Sugihara, and Kenichi Sugihara, of SelectBooks for their help and support.

The
Fundable
Startup

CHAPTER 1

Introduction

"A startup is in reality a 'faith-based enterprise' on day one. To turn the vision into reality and the faith into facts (and a profitable company), a startup must test those guesses, or hypotheses, and find out which are correct."

—Steve Blank, *The Four Steps to the Epiphany*

Have You Dreamed of Starting Your Own Company?

Do you have an idea that could solve an important problem or make the world a better place?

Perhaps you have invented a device, technology, or drug that could address a huge market if you could turn it into a product.

Or, perhaps you've been inspired by the success of people like Bill Gates, founder of Microsoft, Steve Jobs, founder of Apple Computer, or Mark Zuckerberg, founder of Facebook. Or, you may have heard stories of entrepreneurs who sat down to lunch with a venture capitalist and walked away with a check for $5 million to launch a startup company. Or maybe you're tired of working for other people, but instead want to be your own boss.

If any of these descriptions fits you, you will want to learn the lessons of this book and read the stories of these entrepreneurs:

- Dr. Jack Edwards, who dreamed of injecting the first fungal vaccine into humans.

- Steve Casselman, who wanted to build the most powerful supercomputer.

- Lori Torres, who saw a way to clean up the packages piling up in the lobbies of large apartment complexes.

- Josh Roach, who imagined a better way to match math tutors with students.

- Shy Pahlevani, who invented a more effective way of reporting crime in the age of the internet.

- Bryon Merade, who saw an opportunity to improve certain devices used by women's health care providers.

What do these entrepreneurs have in common? They all found a way to get their companies funded. Their simple secret? They built companies that appealed to investors.

Did each of these entrepreneurs serve as the CEO of their company? No! Some did, but many did not. What matters is that they built a "fundable startup," a company that was attractive enough that investors wrote checks.

Important Messages

In *The Fundable Startup*, we will answer these questions:

What does it mean to build a fundable startup?

What are the characteristics of a fundable startup?

How would you create one?

Is there a recipe for success?

This book is not meant to be a recipe for making you a successful CEO. Instead, it provides a strategy for turning a good idea into a successful business. This can involve recruiting a "founder team" of implementers and creating value that will then attract an even stronger management team and a CEO capable of bringing capital to the company.

The situation is straightforward:

Investors are always looking for promising startup companies in which to invest.

Investors have a lot of startups from which to choose. Most venture capitalists (often referred to as "VCs") say they invest in about one out of every one hundred companies they see.

The challenge is how to become the one in one hundred that gets funded. It's simple: you must have the best idea and the strongest management team.

Easier said than done? Of course! One of the purposes of this book is to help the founders of a startup create a company that will attract the capital required to be successful, rather than having to go out and beg for it.

Who Should Lead a Startup?

Writing in *The Atlantic* in 2011, law professor James Kwak suggested that "founders make the best leaders."[1] Kwak called this theory "Steve Jobs's Law," referring to the "superstar CEO" of Apple and citing how that company's performance suffered when executives with more traditional management backgrounds took over.

Some of the best high-tech startups were founded by visionary leaders who managed their companies to enormous success. This includes companies like Hewlett-Packard, Microsoft, Apple, Facebook, Google, and Intel. But, in my experience, these companies are the exception to the rule. Too many good ideas are wasted by leaders who don't know how to turn these ideas into viable businesses. And experienced venture capitalists prefer to invest in companies run by management teams with proven success in similar businesses.

So, who is the best leader for a startup company? The company founder or an experienced CEO and management team? There are good reasons that venture capitalists put a high premium on the proven track record of a management team. My experience with about 150 companies certainly supports this conclusion. We will examine several case studies and some simple logic. The ultimate question, of course, is whether management teams with a history of success are more likely to receive venture capital funding than founders and first-time CEOs.

I believe that companies with experienced management teams are much more likely to succeed than companies led by novice CEOs. The reasons are simple: The skill set of a seasoned CEO is extensive. It generally takes at least fifteen years of experience for an executive to become a qualified CEO.

Here are some of the skills an experienced CEO should have:

- Strategic planning (long range)
- Corporate planning (operational)
- Competitive analysis
- Hiring Personnel
- Supervising personnel
- Dismissing personnel
- Team building
- Complex problem solving
- Working with a board of directors
- Working with lawyers
- Financial analysis
- Developing finance strategy and valuing companies
- Negotiating

These skills are explained in more detail in chapter 8.

Is it surprising that a first time CEO is unlikely to have the skills needed to build a successful company? No. Why, then, would a professional investor risk valuable capital on a founder who has few, or no, CEO credentials?

Venture capitalists lean toward the most compelling—and well-developed—ideas and proven management teams. They are professionals. Why take any more risk than is necessary? Given that they usually have many highly qualified companies from which to choose, they certainly do not need to compromise.

Again, venture capitalists look for CEOs with at least fifteen–twenty years of experience. This book will not offer shortcuts for obtaining that experience. Rather, it describes a method for getting fundable management involved in a startup company in order to maximize the opportunity for success. There are many ways for an inexperienced founder to assemble a team that will attract capital to his company.

The Startup Challenge

Assuming you have an idea for a fundable startup, your challenge is to put the necessary management in place. This is where it gets tricky. Venture capitalists typically work with companies with the best ideas and the most experienced CEOs and management teams. So why would they invest in anything less? The ultimate challenge for most startups is, "Do we have a fundable management team, and, if not, how do we get one?" We address this question in detail in chapter 12.

Startups are complicated, and there are many ways that they can fail. The odds of raising capital are probably akin to the chances of drawing a pair of aces from a 52-card deck (which are one chance in 221 draws). Venture capitalists say they invest in one of every one hundred companies they see, and many companies don't make enough progress to even get their attention.

The essential ingredients of a successful startup are straightforward:

> A disruptive product or service concept
>
> An experienced management team
>
> Adequate financing

The challenge is that the necessary ingredients are intricately interrelated. They form a mesh of stubborn "chicken and egg" problems. The founder must answer questions like:

- How do I get money without a product or a management team?
- How do I build a founder team without money?
- How do I create a product without money?
- How do I create a product without help?
- How do I get help without money?
- How do I hire a CEO without money?
- How do I get money without a CEO?

The instinctive approach of many founders is to write a business plan and approach investors. This rarely works, because the investor has little visibility into the details of the product or the management team. Investors are being asked to accept the risk that the company will develop a winning product and hire a strong management team, which is too much uncertainty for most investors.

The challenge for the leader of a startup company is to navigate the chicken and egg problems with a sequence of small, manageable steps. The trick is to develop the management team and the product as thoroughly as possible before approaching investors. This "bootstrapping" method enables some startups to create a management team, build a product, and recruit an experienced

CEO before approaching investors, thereby greatly improving their chances of obtaining capital.

Important Definitions

The word "disruptive" and the phrase "high tech" have specific meanings in this book.

Disruptive

We use disruptive to describe a new product or service idea that has the potential to dramatically change the way something is done, or the way a problem is solved. Some of the best recent examples would be Federal Express, Dell Computer, Amazon, Facebook, and Google. All of these companies made significant changes in the way we do something important—so important that they defined new industries, or redefined old ones. These are the kinds of businesses that venture capitalists seek out.

Most of the principles described here also apply to businesses that are not disruptive, as well. Some attractive businesses will not be exciting enough to capture the attention of venture capitalists, and some businesses will succeed without venture capital.

Not all fundable ideas will be as dramatic as Amazon or Federal Express, but for an idea to be attractive to investors, it must:

- Promise significant and lasting change.

- Solve an important problem.

- Have the potential for substantial financial return to investors. There are no hard and fast revenue or profit targets for a disruptive business, but investors often use numbers like $100 million or $1 billion in annual revenues to make the point that they want to build substantial companies.

Do all disruptive companies satisfy these criteria? Of course not, but someone probably *thought* they had the potential to do so. We will explore these ideas in chapter 7: The Fundable Idea.

Whether you have a top idea, or not, is largely a question of fact. Does your idea solve a significant problem? Does market research support that there will be a lot of buyers? Will customers pay a price that permits the company to be profitable? These kinds of questions can be answered, precisely or approximately, by thorough market analysis.

High Tech

Throughout this book we use the phrase high tech in its broadest sense to refer to businesses that rely heavily on technology for their competitive advantage. Here, high tech can refer to traditional computer and electronics-related businesses, but also to businesses based on software, the internet, apps, as well as healthcare-related technologies, including medical devices, medical equipment, biotechnology, and medical diagnostic and therapeutic devices or drugs.

Avoiding the Trash Bin

Resourceful entrepreneurs start new businesses all the time and turn them into huge successes. But in the world of high-tech startups, where venture capital funding is almost always necessary, I see an enormous amount of waste. Waste in the sense that disruptive and fundable ideas often fail to get out of the starting gate, because company founders do not have the experience required to raise the necessary capital.

For people who are involved in the startup company funding process, this is not a surprise. Everyone understands that venture capitalists—the primary source of capital for startup companies, after friends and family—try to invest in management teams that have previous successes in their industry. This disqualifies 90 percent of founders, if not more.

If there is a mystery here, it is that the gazillions of incubators, mentors, finders, and job coaches who support them, either are not aware of the realities or they choose to ignore them in hopes of collecting some fees along the way.

Any entrepreneur who is considering managing a high-tech startup, or who works closely with one or more high-tech startups, should learn the messages of this book. It may help her avoid some of the common mistakes that founders make, and, even better, it may help her see a path to creating a company that truly attracts capital.

Why Do I Hold These Views?

My conclusions are based on forty-six years of experience as a venture-capital fund manager, corporate strategic planning executive, angel investor, founding CEO or chairman of five companies, and a director of over twenty companies. I know what investors are looking for and what it takes to build a successful company. I have hired ten CEOs and replaced six, and I have experienced the successes of the experienced and the failures of the inexperienced. More significantly, I have helped a handful of companies bridge the gap to a management team capable of attracting capital.

My psychologist friend and business associate Dr. Donovan Greene calls me a harbor pilot. He says, "You get ships into safe harbor, because you know where the shoals, shipwrecks, and threatening rocks lie." That's a pretty good description of what I do in my daily work. I'm often trying to find a way to keep a company alive and growing until it can find a management team capable of raising capital.

For example, in 2003 Ken Trevett, the CEO of Harbor-UCLA Research and Education Institute (now named Los Angeles Biomedical Research Institute or LA BioMed), asked me to help

Dr. Jack Edwards, head of the infectious diseases department at the institute, to commercialize some of his ideas. Dr. Edwards's department had four interesting technologies, so the first task was to analyze market opportunities and competitive potential for each of the four potential products. After a few months of analysis, it became clear that the vaccine for candida and staph (MRSA) had the potential for revenues in excess of $1 billion per year, a minimum to attract the attention of the major pharmaceutical companies.

For the next few years, I supervised the creation of a business plan and the formation of a corporation called NovaDigm Therapeutics, Inc. I negotiated a license with LA BioMed so that NovaDigm could build a business around several of its patents. We also hired a vice president of research and development. In 2008 we received a commitment for $18 million in venture capital from Domain Associates, one of the top biotech venture capital firms, and in 2009 we recruited an experienced vaccine CEO, Dr. Tim Cooke, to take over the operation of the company. Tim is still running NovaDigm, which recently completed a successful Phase II clinical trial. This process is described in more detail in a case study in chapter 12.

This process illustrates one way that startup founders can resolve the most difficult chicken and egg problem. It's difficult to hire an experienced management team without capital, and it's difficult to attract capital without an experienced management team. In NovaDigm's case, I was the bridge to an experienced CEO. Tim would not have joined NovaDigm before we raised capital, and Domain would probably not have invested had I not been there to build a bridge to an experienced management team.

Unlike most books on entrepreneurial startups, this is not a how to book. At least, it's not a "how-to-be-a-CEO" book. It's more about how to attract a fundable management team and CEO. This book describes ways that an inexperienced founder can find the right management team for his company and greatly increase his chances of attracting capital.

This notion of *attracting* capital is a key message of this book. The premise is that investors are in the business of investing in attractive propositions. They actively seek profitable investment opportunities. So if a company has a truly attractive proposition— that is, a disruptive idea as defined earlier and a proven management team—it should be able to *attract* investors, instead of having to pound the pavement to *sell* investors on a plan.

It is important for the reader to know not just what I believe about high-tech startups, but also why I hold these beliefs and how I arrived at them. I've included some personal experiences like the one below to show how my career evolved from mathematician to computer scientist to strategic planner to venture capitalist to angel investor, and finally, to company founder. One theme of this book is that good careers evolve; they rarely involve a quick leap forward or abrupt changes in direction. A CEO whose career has passed through many learning stages will probably be a better startup company leader than a founder who jumped from a laboratory or technical assignment into a leadership role.

Serving on over twenty boards of directors of high-tech companies has taught me much of what works and what does not work. On many of the boards there were at least two venture capitalists, which led me to appreciate the value that an experienced VC can add. Very few people get the breadth of experience that venture capitalists obtain by serving on the board of directors of as many as ten companies at a time and, of course, many more over a number of years.

Most venture capitalists have an extremely broad range of experience in investing in management teams and working with them. They often provide important strategic guidance to their portfolio companies, and they assist in obtaining additional funding and arranging for exits. It's difficult to imagine another occupation where an individual obtains as much exposure to a broad spectrum of business issues. Consultants, mentors, and advisers work with multiple companies, but, unlike venture capitalists, their reward is not usually tied to the success of their clients.

Getting Started

As we begin our journey, let's explore one of the overriding aspects of almost all high-tech startups: Founders often believe that "if you build a better mousetrap, the world will beat a path to your door." This statement, it turns out, is a misquote of Ralph Waldo Emerson.

> " If a man has good corn or wood, or boards, or pigs, to sell, or can make better chairs or knives, crucibles or church organs, than anybody else, you will find a broad hard-beaten road to his house, though it be in the woods. "
>
> —Ralph Waldo Emerson,
> from entry on "common fame" in *Journal*, 1855

Time after time, the inventors I meet describe their inventions in esoteric, jargon-laden terms, and they assume that the benefits of their inventions are obvious to all. Unfortunately, in this world of computer chips, internet apps, and biopharmaceuticals, the opposite is usually true: Inventions are obscure and difficult to understand. And it takes a lot of work to communicate how they might be translated into products with practical benefits.

The inventor/founder's task is not to wait for the world to beat a path to her door. Her challenges are to explain to the world why her invention matters and to convince investors that she can turn it into a viable commercial business. She needs to use all of her communication and presentation skills to create an extremely effective business plan.

Perhaps the reason so many founders underestimate the task is that they start with the assumption that their idea and its advantages should be obvious to all. Therefore, it never occurs to them that their real challenge is to develop a proof of concept and learn to describe the concept in a compelling way to a nonscientific audience of interested venture capitalists.

> **Leadership is the capacity to translate vision into reality.**
>
> —Warren Bennis, quoted in
> *Executive's Portfolio of Model Speeches for All Occasions*

Turning vision into reality is precisely where the need for leadership arises. Describing the invention clearly for the layman usually reaches beyond a word-smithing exercise. Experienced startup company leaders understand the necessity of assembling a team, creating business plans, developing a prototype product, and getting first customers without investment capital, if possible. The leader's first responsibility is to find a way through this maze, and experience helps.

Good career paths are based on a gradual process of learning and developing skills as an employee discovers his interests and expands his capabilities and competencies. At every step of a career if a person is doing things he enjoys doing and learning important new business lessons, he is likely to advance in a positive direction. Each of these steps will probably take twelve to twenty-four months, if not more.

When I review a resume, if I see multiple job changes in fewer than eighteen months, I get the impression that the candidate is more interested in advancement then in performing well at a given level. This is another argument against a founder jumping from the laboratory to a CEO chair. It defies gravity. It is a giant leap across multiple levels of management and it puts the founder, the company, and the employees at unnecessary risk.

What's in This Book?

The Fundable Startup will answer the question: What is leadership in a startup company, and who can be the best leader?

We'll dig into whether CEOs make the best leaders, looking at the logic of the premise, and some examples. We'll also examine how fragile a high-tech startup company can be and how easy it is for an inexperienced manager to inadvertently destroy the company he is trying to build.

This book's message is not that first-time leaders and management teams cannot succeed. Some will, but the odds are stacked heavily against them. The point is that the odds favor an approach of gradually building value in a startup and attracting as many experienced people as possible.

Here is a summary of the book's remaining chapters:

Chapter 2: High-Tech Gold How important are high-tech startups? What value do they have, and how many jobs do they create?

Chapter 3: Learning from the 99 Percent What can we learn from the startup companies that fail? Why do they fail? How can new startups avoid their mistakes? One key chicken and egg problem: How do I hire a management team without capital; how do I get capital without a management team?

Chapter 4: Creating, Measuring, and Increasing Value The goal of all high-tech startups is to create value. How is value defined, created, and measured?

Chapter 5: Startup Capital: Recent History How do capital markets affect a company's ability to raise capital? What recent trends have influenced capital markets, and what effect have they had on startup companies?

Chapter 6: Venture Capital Think Who are the venture capitalists? How do they think about investments in startup companies?

Chapter 7: The Fundable Idea What kind of business concept is required to attract venture capital to a startup company? What do venture capitalists mean by a disruptive idea?

Chapter 8: The Fundable Management Team What is a fundable management team? What experience do venture capitalists look for in the CEOs of their portfolio companies?

Chapter 9: Where Do Experienced CEOs Come From? How do the best CEOs and managers develop their skills? Why does it often take fifteen–twenty years to obtain the necessary skills?

Chapter 10: Is There a CEO Fast Track? First-time founders have many options for shortening the fifteen–twenty years required to be an experienced CEO. Some are coaches, mentors, incubators, accelerators, to name a few. Do they work?

Chapter 11: Angel Think Who are the angel investors? How do they decide where to invest their capital?

Chapter 12: The Solution: Be a Money Magnet Ways to bootstrap a company and avoid the problems of raising capital without top management, and getting top management without capital. This chapter also addresses technology transfer and methods for creating successful spinout companies.

Chapter 13: Follow the Leader Wrapping up. The formula for startup success is to marry an experienced high-tech management team with a powerful and disruptive idea.

A successful startup is a carefully matched combination of a winning idea with an effective management team and the capital needed to make it all work. The flow of the chapters is intended to explain how to bring the parts together with an emphasis on how important the experience of the management team can be.

But first, in order to understand the demands on the leaders of a startup company, we need to understand why high-tech startup companies are so important in today's economy.

CHAPTER 2

High-Tech Gold

"I am a big believer that technology shapes mankind."

—Mukesh Ambani, Profit NDTV

Why Care About Startups?

Why should we care about startup companies? How important are they to our society and our business culture? Let's see what role they play in our system of capitalism and why we should care about the effectiveness of the startup process.

High-tech startup companies provide value to our economic system in a number of ways:

- The creation of jobs
- The creation of technology
- Improved productivity
- Bringing dreams to life
- The creation of wealth
- The creation of new leaders

Job creation

According to a 2013 Kauffman Foundation research report, high-tech startups create a disproportionate number of new jobs in the US economy. This report shows that high-tech companies fewer than ten years old create jobs at a substantially higher rate than other private companies. They make a significant contribution to new jobs in the United States. These high-tech startups create new jobs and new wealth, but they also make substantial contributions to information and communications technology as well as electronics, software, and health care.[1]

According to an article in *Entrepreneur* magazine, there are between 25 million and 27 million small businesses in the United States that account for 60 to 80 percent of all U.S. jobs.[2]

Since 1980, according to an SBA (Small Business Administration) report, roughly 800–900 thousand new startup companies have been formed each year, including traditional high-tech companies (computer-related hardware), information and communications technology, and health care-related companies.[3]

Startup companies and small business are important creators of employment.

Creation of Technology

Writing about a study by Paychex, a payroll services company, *Forbes* reported that small businesses produce thirteen times more patents than larger firms.[4]

In a 1999 appearance before the Joint Economic Committee of Congress, Federal Reserve Chairman Alan Greenspan observed that "something special has happened to the American economy in recent years. An economy that twenty years ago seemed to have seen its better days, is displaying a remarkable run of economic growth that appears to have its roots in ongoing advances in technology."[5]

Improvements in Productivity

Advances in technology are intricately tied to improvements in all-important productivity measures of a society. The term "technical progress function" is defined as "an economic relation which seeks to explain changes in the level of economic output in terms of the level of technical progress."[6] Rather than looking at economic growth as a form of efficiently allocating inputs, the technical progress function explains economic growth in terms of investment in technological progress. According to an article published by the Dallas Federal Reserve Board, "Technological progress is the only source of sustained labor productivity growth."[7]

We don't have to look very far to see technologies that have had enormous impact on productivity. Consider, for example, the computer, the internet, the smartphone, the driverless vehicle, and the discovery of the structure of DNA.

Bringing Dreams to Life

While financial gain is certainly a motive for most company founders, their dreams are sometimes dominated by other goals. I have worked directly with about fifty startup companies, and I believe every founder had a vision or a dream that he or she passionately wanted to see realized.

- Steve Casselman dreamed of creating the most powerful computer in the world.

- Dr. Jack Edwards dreamed of someday using his vaccines for candidiasis and staph (MRSA) to prevent life-threatening infections in people.

- Josh Roach envisioned a worldwide math tutoring network capable of matching students with the best tutors and providing tools for effective online tutoring sessions.

- Lori Torres saw the need for a better way to manage parcel delivery at residential apartment or condo complexes, and she invented a computer- and internet-based system of lockers for solving the problem.

- Bryon Merade was in the surgical products distribution business, and he saw an opportunity to deliver much improved materials and tools.

- Corinne Wong developed a method for time releasing drugs into the retina with the potential for helping to cure advanced macular degeneration and diabetic retinopathy.

- Drs. Greg Mason and John Michael Criley, looking at patient monitoring readouts, saw a way to detect cardiac tamponade, a life-threatening condition, in time to save lives.

- Chuck Drexel, one of the top mass flow controller engineers in the world, saw a way to build an even better controller using fewer and cheaper parts.

Not all of these ideas turned out to be blockbuster business opportunities, but they represent the kinds of dreams that fuel startup companies and their founders, and ultimately improve the quality of life for people throughout the world.

Turning dreams into reality usually comes at a cost. It is not unusual for a startup company to require millions or tens of millions of dollars in order to bring a product to market. Venture capital is the life blood of startup companies. Its free flow is a critical ingredient for the success of startups.

Creation of Wealth

The founders of many startup companies try to emulate the success of famous companies like Hewlett-Packard, Intel, Microsoft, Amgen, Apple, Google, and Facebook. Every entrepreneur knows the success model: The founder creates a company, gets a funding commitment over lunch from a top venture capital firm, achieves early success, and takes the company public at an enormous valuation, making himself, his cofounders, his family and friends and his investors extremely wealthy!

When venture capitalists or other investors invest in a company, they usually make their return on investment when the company is acquired by another company or when the company registers to sell its stock in an Initial Public Offering (IPO). An IPO can also be an opportunity for founders and employees to cash in their stock or stock options—hopefully at a profit. One of the most impressive examples, according to a 2005 article in the *New York Times* is the 1986 Microsoft IPO, which created "approximately 10,000 Microsoft millionaires" by the year 2000.[8] According to Appleinsider, Apple's IPO on December 12, 1980 instantly created 300 millionaires.[9]

Creation of New Leaders

Startups provide an extraordinary opportunity for experienced leaders to sharpen their skills and tackle even broader management challenges. We are not advocating for founders to jump from the laboratory or classroom into a leadership role. But when a qualified leader joins a startup, she can build many layers of new and valuable knowledge on top of her previous experience, thereby qualifying to either take the startup to a higher level or to move into a CEO role with a larger company.

More about Job Creation

According to the Small Business Administration, the catch in the impressive number of jobs created by startups is that, in many years, the number of jobs lost due to closures is only slightly fewer than the number of jobs created by new startups. In fact, during the downturn economic cycle of 2008–2010, the number of jobs lost due to closures exceeded the number of new jobs created by startups.[3]

Conclusion

While startup companies are formed for a variety of reasons, all have the potential to create wealth and jobs and to greatly improve some aspect of our lives. Moreover, all face significant challenges.

This leads us to the fundamental issue this book addresses: How can we improve the efficiency of the startup process, so that the number of jobs created will grow faster than the number of jobs lost due to closures?

To gain a better understanding of the problems, in chapter 3: "Learning from the 99 Percent," we will examine why the majority of startups fail to meet their objectives.

CHAPTER 3

Learning from the 99 Percent

"Success doesn't teach as many lessons as failure does."

—Jay Samit, *Disrupt You!*

The Odds of Success

It is estimated that as many as 90 percent of high-tech startups fail. In my experience, the percentage may be even greater, because I see companies in their very early stages—before incorporation, fundraising, and launch. Many of these companies never incorporate, never raise their first dollar, and never develop a product.

What can the founder of a new high-tech venture learn from these failures?

- Are there known routes to success?
- Are there patterns of failure?
- Are there approaches to avoid?

Many venture capitalists say they invest in one out of every one hundred deals they see. One source says the number is one out of every four hundred.[1]

But even if we assume that the higher number get funding, when we consider that only one out of ten of those will succeed, the odds of hitting a home run are pretty slim.

Here's another way to think about it. Imagine that you are a venture capitalist with one hundred business plans on your desk. You have scored each of the plans on a scale from one to ten with respect to both the strength of the management team and the business potential of the concept. Which plan do you choose? Obviously, the one that scored ten on both counts, if there is one. Why should you settle for anything less?

What if that deal doesn't work out? Most venture capitalists would not select a plan with the idea rated nine and the management team rated ten, because it is unlikely that the management team will be able to turn the concept into a ten.

But companies with a score less than ten for the management team might have a chance, because there are several options for improving the management score to a ten:

- Surround the team with good coaching.
- Add one or more new members to the team to fill in gaps or change the dynamic.
- Take a chance with the management team and deal with problems later if necessary.

Each venture capitalist will have a unique perception, so the odds of getting a company funded may actually be better than one in one hundred. Even so, the hurdle is still very high. To emphasize this point throughout this book, we refer to the "1 percent," figuratively, as the companies with a reasonable chance of getting venture capital funding, and the "99 percent" as the companies that are likely to struggle to get any funding.

Where Does It Go Wrong?

Researchers have tried to determine the reasons that so many startups fail.

One study of 3,200 failed startup companies showed that 70 percent of them simply tried to scale up their businesses too rapidly.[2] This is a typical mistake of inexperienced company founders. In their eagerness to be successful, they take whatever capital is available, even if it is not enough to allow the company to meet its important milestones.

The website Statistic Brain published a list of "leading management mistakes."[3] Patricia Schaeffer, a writer and former staff member for Business Know-How, wrote an article identifying seven reasons for failure.[4] Here is a combination of the reasons they cited:

1. Going into business for the wrong reasons

2. Taking advice from family and friends

3. Being in the wrong place at the wrong time

4. Family pressure on time and money commitments

5. Pride

6. Lack of market awareness

7. Falling in love with the product/business

8. Lack of financial responsibility and awareness

9. Lack of clear focus

10. Lack of planning

11. Poor management

12. Too much money

13. Not enough money

14. Getting worn out or underestimating the time requirements

15. Overexpansion

These are mistakes that sneak up on entrepreneurs and founders. Of course, founders start with every intention of being successful. Many, though, do not have the analytic tools to know if they are going into business for the right reasons, or if they are in the right place at the right time. Many are willing to take advice from others, but they listen to inexperienced advisers, and they get bad recommendations. Many founders underestimate the time (and effort) required to build a successful business.

In the category of "going into business for the wrong reasons" are (1) a need for a salary and (2) a desire to be one's own boss. If a founder is in desperate need of an income, he should get a paying job. Pressure to raise capital can force a startup into a series of fatal strategies.

A desire to be one's own boss can be a motivating factor for an entrepreneur who wants to start a new company. A founder might want more responsibility or an opportunity to get out from under the control of an oppressive boss. But if a CEO simply wants to operate unconstrained, he might be in for a surprise.

In a healthy startup, the CEO usually ends up reporting to the board of directors and, if the board of directors is doing its job in leading the company, it has not just the ability, but the obligation to shareholders to direct the CEO and replace him if they deem it necessary. If your goal is to be your own boss, this scenario may not be a good answer. The CEO of a successful startup company has multiple bosses in the form of the directors, and, if the board is doing its job, it is a tough taskmaster.

It's probably not possible to get meaningful statistics about high-tech failures. Most companies that fail simply evaporate. They run out of cash and the founders and employees quietly move to other projects. There's no pathologist standing by to perform an autopsy. Even if there were, the reasons for failure would be highly subjective. Why did the company run out of capital? Did it spend too fast? Were sales too slow to materialize. Did the company have the wrong sales personnel? Did the product fail to perform as advertised? Did it really solve a common problem, which would cause consumers to seek it out? Was it priced properly? It is very difficult to know exactly why a startup ran out of money

Can these mistakes be avoided? I believe that many of them can be, but it takes the expertise of experienced professionals. Even then, success is not guaranteed. Deborah Gage, a reporter for the *Wall Street Journal*, quotes research by Shikhar Ghosh, a senior lecturer at Harvard Business School, that concludes, "Three out of four venture capital-backed companies fail," and that the rate may be even higher depending on how failure is defined. These are companies that were able to raise venture capital, so you would think they might succeed. It is commonly thought that a startup fails if it does not return the funds invested by the venture capitalists. But if this is the case, then the overall failure rate actually may be as high as 95 percent.[5]

There are many analyses of why companies fail. But, in my experience, there is one common theme: *they run out of money*. Many would continue to operate if they still had money in the bank. There may be some exceptions, but few companies shut down when they still have funds.

The important question is, "Why did they run out of money, and why didn't they raise more?" In their rush to get funded, many companies either underestimate the amount of capital they need, or they accept an amount that is not sufficient to achieve significant value-increasing and risk-reducing milestones. A startup needs to carefully plan its capital needs and how it will use that capital.

We might wonder why a startup team does not raise more money in the first place. Possible reasons are:

> They didn't know how much they really needed.
>
> They took the capital that was available without checking to see if it was really enough.

They burned through their funding faster than expected.

All of these reasons.

Any way you slice it, if a company runs out of money, it didn't have enough initially. Did the company realistically assess its capital needs and overspend its budget? Or did it underestimate its capital requirements? Sometimes, unforeseen events cause a company to overspend its budget. These can be mishaps that could not reasonably have been expected to occur. Possible causes of an income shortfall could be a delayed product introduction, poor product sales, or an inability to charge the planned price for the product. Examples of excessive spending could include unexpected sales costs, higher than expected product costs, or higher than forecasted marketing costs. In a sense, this is a distinction without a difference. A sound estimate of capital requirements should include contingency for unforeseen events.

However, it is common for a startup to overestimate projected revenues and underestimate projected expenses. In their enthusiasm, founders can be overly optimistic about how quickly their product will be accepted by customers. And, as much as they might try to anticipate every expense, it is extremely difficult to think of everything that has to be done. It is almost impossible to precisely assess how much effort will be required, how long it will take, and how much it will cost.

The ability to realistically forecast revenue, expenses, and capital needs can be the factor that separates successful—and therefore "fundable"—CEOs from inexperienced ones. In one way or another, it explains why most startup companies fail.

The Fragile Startup

As an energetic golf aficionado, I see a striking similarity between the golf swing and a successful startup company.

Both have many moving parts that have to fit together smoothly for things to work well. In the golf swing, the swing plane, backswing path, position at the top of the swing, hips, torso, shoulders, arms, hands, club face, and "angle of attack" must all be balanced. If the parts don't work together, the result is likely to be a disaster. Startup companies share a similar dynamic: The basic concept, business strategy, product plan, sales and marketing plan, management team, CEO, financing strategy, board of directors, and investors must all "fit together" like a well-tuned golf swing.

Unfortunately, the statistics don't tell us about the thousands of companies that fail before they get launched. Frequently, a founder will invent a product and immediately write a business plan and start talking to investors. Investors invest in companies, generally not just in either founders (unless they are Steve Jobs or Bill Gates) or ideas no matter how promising they are. A company with no product, no customers, and no management team has very little chance of attracting enough capital to succeed.

The bottom line is that the process of establishing a winning startup is difficult, and a founder must do everything in his power to maximize the chance of success.

The ability to realistically forecast revenue, expenses, and capital needs can be the factor that separates successful—and therefore "fundable"—CEOs from inexperienced ones. In one way or another, it explains why most startup companies fail.

A startup can employ two strategies: one that may lead to success and one that will most certainly lead to failure. First is a strategy based on the company raising enough capital to meet predetermined milestones. These milestones will add significant value to the company and reduce the company's risk to investors.

The idea is that each financing stage should add enough value, and eliminate enough risk, to make the next financing attractive to investors at a higher share price. Companies don't always get that higher price, but the basic strategy can be a key to survival.

The second strategy is the converse of one based on mile-stones. Instead, the company plans to build a bridge "halfway across the river." This refers to a company not raising enough capital to achieve significant milestones. In this case, they face two very serious, often fatal, challenges: They have to go back to investors for more capital without having increased their value, or stock price, and they have to go back to investors having failed to meet the objectives of the original business plan. This creates doubt in the mind of investors. "Can this team execute its plans?" Companies in this situation often find it impossible to raise additional capital. This is a common cause for failure of startup companies, and it is one of the most frequently made mistakes of inexperienced founders.

Too many high-tech startups with promising ideas fail because the founder makes mistakes that cause the company to run out of capital prematurely. The founder might not truly understand what it takes to obtain the funding her company will need to be successful.

So Many Ways to Fail

There are many more ways for a startup to go wrong than to go right. Most have financial implications, but not all are related to money. An inexperienced founder is likely to get blind-sided by a mistake he did not see coming. Many miscalculations involve time because it ends up taking longer than expected to complete important tasks. Inexperienced founders often underestimate how long it will take to hire people. They underestimate the time they will spend resolving unexpected personnel issues. They underestimate how long it will take to negotiate strategic partnerships. They underestimate how long it will take to develop a new product. They underestimate how long it will take to test and then sell that product. They overestimate how soon they will be paid for the sale of their product. They are very slow to consult lawyers and accountants, so they end up getting into unexpected legal problems.

One reason that inexperienced founders might try to manage their own companies is that they do not believe that a seasoned manager would have the same passion about their vision. They may be right. An "imported" professional manager, far from the original invention or concept, is likely to be less passionate about it. But in most cases, it is exactly what the startup needs. That experienced CEO is more likely to look at the concept dispassionately through the lens of significant business experience. While this might be disconcerting to the passionate founder, it's actually a necessary part of the process of building a successful company.

A founder's passion and persistence can be very positive qualities for a startup company, but unless they are shaped by business realities, they can interfere with the company-building process.

Some startup company leaders do not seem to understand how important it is to create a "proof of concept"—a working model, prototype, or first version of the company's product that demonstrates that the product will work and can be built for the expected cost. This is a necessary step in order to attract investors and strategic partners. Very few investors or partners are willing to take the risk of funding a project that is still in the research stage. They see it as too risky for their investment style. Funding for proof of concept is a sort of financial no-man's land. In industries where government grants are available, they can save the day, but they are never easy to access. But, in general, a great deal of focus is required to clear this important hurdle.

Reasons That Startups Fail

Experienced and successful startup company CEOs understand that there are tried and true methods for building a startup company. Inexperienced CEOs and founders generally do not know the tried and true approaches. They try to invent their own approaches, sometimes with disastrous results. Here are some classic reasons why a company can fail. Remember that failure is like a snake in the grass, which can pop up and bite you at any time if you don't know what to look for.

Fear That Professional Management Will Mess Things Up

Recently a first-time CEO told me, "I'm the only person who can run this company." His message was that he had the best understanding of the technology, and he had a personal relationship with each member of the management team and that he understood exactly what each team member was supposed to accomplish. The message I get is that the new CEO does not really understand that there are proven techniques of management that would allow an experienced CEO from the outside to walk into this situation, get to know the people, get to know the company's objectives, and effectively manage the company.

Every founder thinks he can be the next Steve Jobs, Bill Gates, David Packard, or Mark Zuckerberg, or he wouldn't take the leap and attempt a startup. These incredible successes are extremely seductive to a budding entrepreneur. They offer the promise that a founder-entrepreneur can build a very successful company and create enormous wealth for the company's founders and investors.

The Mistaken Belief that the CEO Has to be an Expert in the Field

One blind spot affecting many founders is the notion that a CEO would have to be a world expert on their company's technology. Let's look at the logic of this philosophy.

If you are building a new restaurant building, which do you hire: a food expert or an architect? Clearly, an architect. The architect doesn't have to know how to make quiche lorraine in order to build a restaurant building. By the same token, a CEO does not have to understand DNA sequences to build a biotech company. The basic building blocks of most companies are similar:

- A corporation, capital structure
- A management team
- Products
- Customers
- Markets
- Competitors
- A business strategy
- A financial strategy
- A business model

Does it help if the CEO understands the technology? Of course. But it is usually possible for a good generalist CEO to build a successful company without extensive domain expertise.

The founding chairman/CEO does not necessarily need detailed knowledge about the company's technology or industry. She can simply be the business organizer. Among the companies that I personally organized without having much knowledge of any of the technologies are a supercomputer company, a biotech company, and a medical device company. There are business fundamentals that work across almost all product/market domains. The fundamentals of creating a legal corporation are the same. The principles of business planning are generic. Measuring markets and competition are relatively technology-agnostic. Industry knowledge, known as domain expertise, is certainly an advantage for a CEO, but a generalist with little domain expertise can build a bridge to a CEO with domain expertise.

Raising Capital Prematurely

Startups have a tendency to try to raise capital before they should. It could be because the founder or team members are desperate for cash to pay their bills. Startups that succumb to these pressures do not usually fare well. They often do not have a complete story to tell. There isn't enough of a team to interest investors. The company has no product, no proof of concept, and no customers. The business plan is not developed in enough detail, or its claims are not supported with enough logic and research. A startup should never be seen as a quick path to paying the bills. If a founder needs a salary immediately, he should probably get a job and deal with the startup later.

It is extremely important to do first things first in approaching fundraising. There is no substitute for a carefully executed step-by-step approach to creating a company that can *attract* capital.

Burning Through Cash Too Quickly

I believe the most common reason for failure of startups is that they either fail to raise capital, or they burn through their capital prematurely. Here's an example of the latter.

One of my companies developed a viable natural voice recognition system in the early 1980s. The system was roughly comparable to today's Dragon Systems product, at least in intent. The founder was able to raise a limited amount of venture capital in order to advance the product to a fairly robust state. As the lead investor for a round of venture capital (about $7 million), I realized that, in order to attract new investors to the financing, we would have to recruit a more experienced CEO.

In retrospect, I would have to say the strategy backfired, but not necessarily for predictable reasons. We were able to raise the $7 million but some of the new investors insisted that the company take the product to market prematurely, presumably to demonstrate its advantages over the Kurzweil medical dictation machine, which had received limited market acceptance at that time. This aggressive marketing strategy depleted the company's cash before it could prove the product's advantages, and the company was forced to retrench.

The company should have kept a lower profile and continued to improve and cost-reduce its product. According to Moore's Law (an observation made by Gordon Moore, one of the cofounders of Intel), which predicts a doubling of capacity and power in computer chips every year or so, the technology would soon be available to produce more powerful hardware platforms. This would make the company's system much more cost-effective within a few years.

Not all startup company mistakes are made by inexperienced founders. Some are made by overaggressive, or inexperienced, investors.

Managing by Democratic Principles

Some founders think a democratic approach involving several team members can substitute for having one experienced leader. This is not surprising in our democratic world. But taking a vote of several people is not a substitute for having a leader who has dealt previously with the issues of starting a new company.

To go back to the harbor pilot analogy no number of intelligent but inexperienced people can substitute for a harbor pilot who knows the location of old shipwrecks, submerged rocks and sandbars.

It would be hard to overstate the importance of this last point. Many company founders are extremely intelligent individuals with advanced degrees and success in their careers. In my experience, intelligence can be a liability if it leads founders to think they can solve business, legal, and accounting problems by themselves. Founders sometimes assume that business decisions are intuitive and easy to make. This assumption is true at times but it can be a trap. Decisions such as the following are not necessarily intuitive:

Corporate structure

Organizational structure

Capital structure

Company valuation

Initial funding requirements

Financial strategy

Startup strategy

Deal structures

Managing by Intuition: Reinventing the Wheel

Here's an example of how inexperienced founders reinventing a wheel can unwittingly put a startup company in jeopardy.

There are two common and legally acceptable methods for distributing stock among the founders of a corporation: One is to sell "founders shares" at a nominal price, possibly with some form of agreement that permits the company to buy back the shares under certain conditions. The second method is to grant stock options to each of the founders; that is, options to purchase shares of stock in the future after they have, presumably, increased in value.

The first method, the purchase of founders' shares, can have some tax advantages to the founders, as they establish a low "basis" price for their shares.

A group of founders that I worked with was extremely concerned about the possibility that one or more members might not pull his weight in the future. So, they designed a mechanism for issuing founder stock in a way that they thought would solve this problem. They decided to sell a portion of the founders' shares upon incorporation and another, roughly equal, portion approximately eighteen months later. The problem with this is that If the shares purchased at the second stage were deemed by the IRS to have a higher value than the original shares, the difference could be taxable to the founders.

A company is formed for the purpose of creating and increasing value, so a claim that no value would be created would be counter to what is supposed to happen. Planning upon incorporation to sell founders' shares eighteen months later at the original price could create an unwanted tax event for the founders. I spoke with four lawyers about this approach, and all four said that it was inadvisable. The founders had no way of knowing upon the company's founding whether the shares would increase in value during the following eighteen to twenty-four months. The founders unwittingly exposed themselves to a potential unwanted tax liability. All of this could have been avoided by following the company's lawyer's advice.

This problem arose because inexperienced founders tried to reinvent the wheel, the process of how founders would be properly compensated. Inexperienced founders too often believe that they are smart enough and creative enough to work through any issues that arise. However, many business solutions are time-tested and have been proven successful. And sometimes they are much more complicated than they appear—especially when taxation is involved.

An experienced CEO who readily takes advice from accountants and lawyers can avoid many of the pitfalls that are likely to trap an inexperienced team.

Using Anecdotal Instead of Systematic Approaches

Experienced CEOs generally approach problems and strategies for solving them in a systematic manner. They identify, evaluate, and explore the options until they arrive at a viable solution to a problem. New CEOs seem to jump at the first alternative that presents itself. This is an "anecdotal" approach because it pursues solutions to a problem one at a time.

For example, NovaDigm Therapeutics hired an executive as its vice president of research that many of the founders knew. All felt that he was well qualified for the job and they offered the position to him without considering other candidates. In this case, the anecdotal approach produced a good result, but it often does not produce the best outcome.

The systematic approach is the opposite of the anecdotal approach. It considers all, or many, alternative solutions to a problem in parallel. For example, NovaDigm Therapeutics hired its CEO by working for some months with one of the top executive recruiting firms in the country. It evaluated approximately 75 potential candidates and finally narrowed the list down to three finalists, one of whom accepted the job. The systematic approach explores many options in parallel. It requires a careful identification of alternatives, and evaluation of each. But it can be slow if it takes weeks to explore each alternative.

While an anecdotal approach might get to a solution faster, the systematic approach is more likely to result in a better and more lasting solution.

Rick Schaffzin was an engineer with a PhD in management. When I helped recruit Rick as CEO of IC Sensors, one of the first things we did was to develop a spreadsheet listing dozens of potential products the company could make with its technology. Each product was evaluated and scored for criteria such as customer demand, market potential, ease of manufacture, technical feasibility, and other criteria. I worked with the company for several months to quantify each of the criteria and select the two most promising products. An experienced CEO is more likely to take this systematic approach to problem solving.

It is understandably human to prefer to deal with people we know rather those we don't know. Perhaps it is because of a certain amount of insecurity, or need for comfort, that many first-time founders adopt an anecdotal approach to problem solving. But the anecdotal approach can lead to failure because it is an inefficient search process, and it often produces results that are less than optimal.

Failure to Properly Vet Vendors

One startup company planned to sell European antiques over the internet to American buyers. Using personal resources, the founder hired a developer to create a "photographic catalog" website to display available furniture pieces. Unfortunately, the site was constructed in a way that made it very difficult to update or improve. Making the same mistake a second time, the founder jumped to another website developer to repackage the site and make significant improvements to its user interface. But the underlying architecture of the website was still flawed and it was both difficult and expensive to make improvements. Because the founder had expended his personal resources in developing a still-unfinished website, he did not have the resources to populate the site with enough product photographs to make his business attractive to customers. This problem could have been avoided if the founder had simply examined the past work of the web developer and talked to a few former customers to determine the quality of his work.

Another hopeful founder used personal resources to pay a web developer to create a website with the ability to attach personal video backgrounds for the sales personnel in an auto dealership. The idea was to personalize the dealership in an effort to make it, and the salespeople, more attractive to customers. After several redesigns, the development efforts had almost exhausted the founder's resources and the company still did not have a viable website. Part of the difficulty, in this case, was that a relatively expensive website was used to validate an untested business concept. This approach can work if an app or website can be created relatively quickly and inexpensively, but inexperienced founders face the risk of an open-ended, never-ending website development project.

There is a simple solution to this problem. Experienced executives learn how to vet vendors. Vetting involves checking a vendor's credentials and references in detail and reviewing previously completed projects. As a result, they are much less likely to have false starts. They are also generally more disciplined at overseeing periodic design and implementation reviews and checkpoints so that, if there are development problems, they are detected early in the process.

Underestimating the Cost of Driving Enough Traffic to a Website

Some business-to-business companies have a chicken-and-egg problem of simultaneously building two kinds of traffic on a website. If they are brokering transactions between buyers and sellers, they need to have enough buyers on the website to make it attractive to sellers and, conversely, they need enough sellers to make the site attractive and "sticky" (visitors stay on the pages) for buyers.

A startup company funded by angel investors was attempting to broker product placement contracts between advertisers and media producers. Their plan was to help product advertisers, such as Coke, find opportunities for product placement in movies and television productions. The other side of the equation was to help movie and TV producers find companies willing to pay to place their products into media productions. Unfortunately, the founders wanted to launch the company with a pricing scheme that would produce early revenue and reduce the company's cash requirements.

But placing any price on the service before the company had a critical mass of buyers and sellers was problematic. The pricing resulted in a lengthy sales discussion that made it difficult for the company to attract either buyers or sellers. The company never achieved the critical mass required to make the website work.

A factor in this company's downfall was that the angel investors provided a relatively small amount of capital—probably too little to sustain the company long enough to make its model work. And the angels were reluctant to put more capital to work. The company may have had a very narrow window of opportunity to succeed, but it would have had to establish a large database of users by giving its service away, in order to prove its concept. Having done that, it might have been able to raise additional capital.

Underestimating Customer Acquisition Costs

One startup company had an appealing business model that involved providing large-company-style buying power to small businesses. The company would negotiate volume purchases with large vendors of office equipment and supplies and make them available to small businesses by means of a reverse auction process in which buyers would post their needs and vendors would bid for the business.

The business model seemed to get off to a good start, and the company raised over $20 million in venture capital for expansion. Unfortunately, the company concluded, after some months of operation, that its cost of bringing potential buyers to the website was too high in relation to the commissions it was able to charge for its services. The board of directors returned the remaining capital to investors and closed the company's doors.

On the internet it's sometimes necessary to almost give away value at the beginning in order to create value in the future. Few companies have implemented the strategy better than Amazon, which made the decision to operate at a lower profitability for a number of years in order to capture eyeballs on its website. Many internet companies have learned that they have to create traffic first and then worry about monetizing their websites.

Almost all of the reasons for failure of startups involve some form of getting the cart before the horse, or somehow doing things out of order. There is a proven sequence of events that will work for a high percentage of startup companies. The key is getting the right people involved at the right time. The optimal sequence goes something like this:

1. Identify the "disruptive" concept.

2. Use stock to recruit a minimal, possibly part-time, implementation team.

3. Develop a demonstration, first product, or proof of concept.

4. Get customer exposure, endorsements, and feedback, if possible.

5. Leverage the strength of your team and value created to attract additional players.

6. Leverage the strength of your team and/or product to attract a "fundable CEO."

7. Attract capital.

This strategy can help a startup slice through a double-chicken-and-egg problem: getting both a team and a CEO without needing significant capital. The initial team helps create value, which helps attract the CEO, which helps attract capital. Some might argue that it's better to recruit the CEO first and let her build the team, but this assumes the startup can attract a qualified CEO without having capital. It is very difficult to attract a top CEO without capital.

The leader of a startup company must have a healthy respect for the task. Most startups do not meet their goals. The leader's attitude should be, "This is a tough task. I'm going to need all the help and advice I can get. I must be smart about getting the right people involved, and I need, with help from my team, to develop a business strategy that gives us a reasonable chance of succeeding."

Conclusion

The best way to avoid the long list of potential potholes that destroy so many startups is to find an experienced CEO to lead the startup. Experience matters. A CEO who has helped to create a successful startup company is unlikely to make the mistakes that cause startups to fail. Sound leadership is a key to success.

The leader of a startup company must know how the value of a company is measured and precisely how to build value in a startup. We will explore these important ideas in chapter 4: "Creating, Measuring and Increasing Value."

Creating, Measuring, and Increasing Value

"Intrinsic value can be defined simply: It is the discounted value of the cash that can be taken out of a business during its remaining life. The calculation of intrinsic value, though, is not so simple. As our definition suggests, intrinsic value is an estimate rather than a precise figure, and it is additionally an estimate that must be changed if interest rates move or forecasts of future cash flows are revised."

—Warren Buffett,
Berkshire Hathaway Inc.: An Owner's Manual (1999)

Valuing Startup Companies

There are two ways to measure value in high-tech startup companies:

Economic value represented by realized profits and cash flows or potential economic value according to reliably forecasted growth in revenue and profits (the Buffett calculation).

Perceived value, future promise, or a "storyline" that promises exceptional profits in the future.

This chapter will explain how value is created, measured, and increased in a high-tech company.

Intrinsic Value

As Warren Buffet suggests, intrinsic, or economic, value is the discounted value of the cash that can be obtained from a business. As a spreadsheet exercise, this usually involves creating a five-year projection of the company's cash flows and an estimated terminal value, which is the net value of the company's assets at the end of the forecast period. These values are then discounted to a present value using an investor's cost of capital as a discount rate. (If you expect to make a 10 percent return on your money, the discounted (present) value of $1 million given to you one year later is $909,090, the amount you would have to invest at 10 percent for one year in order to receive $1 million after one year.)

A discounted value, or net present value (NPV) of a company's cash flows is fairly straightforward, and, according to studies, it has the best chance of correlating with stock market valuations. An NPV model is simply a discounting of cash inflows and outflows expected in the future, usually with some additional value in the final year for the company's estimated terminal value. This stream of cash flows is discounted at the investor's desired return on investment in order to produce a net present value. This process can be performed simply by using the NPV function in most contemporary spreadsheet applications. To discount one year's value to the previous year's value, you divide the future year's value by the number 1 plus the discount rate.

This is the process that sophisticated investors use to value startup companies, using a discount rate in the range of 60-80 percent. These calculations almost always lead to startup company valuations in the range of $1.5 million to $3 million. This surprises many entrepreneurs, but it's just math. It's the result of discounting the cash flows and terminal value of a company with $50-$100 million in projected revenue, with reasonable profit margins and return on capital, over a five-year period. Building a good NPV model forces a company to think through major issues and assumptions:

- What resources will be required?
- What capital will be required?
- What investment return do our investors seek?
- What would be a reasonable valuation for the company?

At TRW Inc., I worked with several senior staff people who had made some important contributions to the subject of "company valuation," or estimating the economic value of a business. They were experts on the subject of net present value and discounted cash flow (DCF) calculations as a method for valuing companies. They had strong evidence that these methods provided the highest correlation to stock market valuations, the ultimate test. I used these methods to help negotiate the sale of the Datacom International and Vidar Transmission Products divisions of TRW. I also used them to determine how to allocate the proceeds of the one sale to approximately 35 different international distribution companies. This could have been a contentious process, but the authority of the DCF model made all 35 entities comfortable.

Perceived Value

Some companies are valued for their future promise regardless of their current revenues, profits, or cash flow. It is not unusual, for example, for biotech or internet companies with exciting prospects, such as a treatment for some form of cancer, to receive extremely high valuations. If a company's product concept is truly exciting, the company might be valued on the basis of future potential, even though it has no revenue or profit numbers on which to base an economic value. This phenomenon of promise is easy to see in the market capitalization of some public high-tech companies today. Companies like Amazon, Facebook, and Google, for example, have had market capitalizations that were not easily justified by current levels of profitability and cash flow. Once a company has a significant financial history, the measure of its valuation is more likely to be based on its financial performance.

Managing Risk and Value

In the early stages of a startup, there is very little value and considerable risk. The primary risks that investors see are:

- Can the product be developed?
- Will the company do what it says it can do?
- Does the company have strong leadership?
- Does the company have a strong management team?
- Can the company create a proof of concept?
- Is there proof that the technology will work?
- Will customers buy the product?
- Will the company be able to raise enough capital?

The startup company's challenge is to find ways to create value and reduce risk within its limited portfolio of resources.

Creation of Value

How is value created or increased? Even before a startup has the ability to produce cash flows, if it can create a virtual team, get to proof of concept, or, even better, develop a product and receive the endorsement of a customer, it will have created value and reduced risk without giving up any equity.

Here are some of the most common steps to add value and/or reduce risk:

- Creating an initial product development team.
- Demonstrating proof of concept.
- Building a product prototype.
- Demonstrating the feasibility of building the product with the specified capabilities and cost.
- Creating the product.
- Getting a first customer.
- Getting a positive customer endorsement.
- Expanding the management team.
- Creating a strong board of directors.
- Obtaining additional customers.
- Obtaining strong customer references.
- Obtaining repeat business from customers.
- Creating a strong online presence.
- Recruiting a fundable CEO.

The secret to creating a successful startup company is to follow a sequence of important steps that can be completed with small amounts of capital, or no capital at all—steps that make the company more attractive to investors and help the company attract the resources it will need to be successful.

This is a milestone-driven approach to attracting capital. As we saw in chapter 3, the idea is to achieve one or more significant milestones that will allow the company to raise its next capital at a higher valuation. Implicit in this strategy is the assumption that the company has enough capital to *complete* the milestones and raise its next round of capital. This is where many companies fail: they either don't raise enough capital to complete the next set of milestones, or they burn through their cash without achieving the milestones.

The Value and Risk Equation

If a management team is doing its job effectively, a company should always be creating additional value for its shareholders. Value is always perceived in relation to risk. If a company's strategy is seen as highly risky, then the value must be perceived as great enough to justify the risk for investors. The actions listed above for increasing value also reduce risk, which is extremely important to investors.

The more startup companies do to increase value and reduce risk, the better their chances of raising capital and the greater their valuation is likely to be. This is the basis for a strategy known as bootstrapping, in which a company operates for as long as possible with little or no capital. The idea, of course, is to reduce risk and increase value as much as possible before raising capital. This greatly improves a company's chances of attracting capital and increasing its valuation for investment purposes.

The important goal, of course, is to move the company forward as far as possible without capital and, then, to raise the smallest amount of capital that will allow the company to continue building value. A successfully implemented bootstrap strategy puts a company in a much stronger position to attract strong team members and capital.

Some companies are not able to bootstrap. The obvious example is a semiconductor company that needs a major investment in manufacturing equipment and facilities before it can produce product. Recently, I met a company that is designing a sophisticated drug-dispensing device, and their startup challenge is that they may need as much as $3 million just to design their machine. The bootstrapping strategy can be a powerful way to launch a startup, but it's very important to identify all startup tasks and make sure they can be accomplished without significant capital.

Managing Cash

> "Happiness is positive cash flow."
>
> —Fred Adler, American venture capitalist and
> author of *Happiness is Positive Cash Flow*

A venture capitalist's worst nightmare is to have a company run out of cash unexpectedly.

One of the most difficult and critical tasks for a startup company CEO is to develop an appropriate and defensible market forecast and business plan in order to determine the company's cash needs. Startup companies habitually overstate their revenue projections and understate their expenses. Because profits and cash flows are the difference between revenues and expenses, errors in either can become greatly magnified, leading to substantial errors in forecasting a company's cash requirements and almost always in the direction of underestimating cash needs.

To better understand this phenomenon, let's look at the problems of forecasting revenues and expenses separately.

The Difficulty of Forecasting Revenues

A startup company's revenue forecast is determined by at least these five key factors:

> When will the product be ready for prime time?
>
> What sales resources will be in place when the product is introduced to its market?
>
> How strong will demand be?
>
> How long will it take to sell the product?
>
> How long will it take to train a new salesperson?

It's easy to be overly optimistic about when a product will be ready for customer sales. Product development cycles are usually longer than anticipated. Companies often underestimate the time required for testing a product, as well as the number of fixes that will be required. One reality of the product development world that most companies underestimate is that a product "fix" often results in a new product "problem." This can cause product development and testing cycles to seem endless. It requires a lot of experience and discipline to produce realistic forecasts for product development and product testing.

In the early days of a product's market life, it is very difficult to know what the sales cycle will be. Frequently, initial sales are made by the inventor himself, who is often the best possible salesperson. It may be difficult to hire independent salespeople who understand the product as well as the inventor and who can be as articulate about it as the inventor. Moreover, initial sales are often made to early innovators and other people who are taking a risk on a newly invented idea. Since the product has no installed base of customers who can be referenced and no basis for comparison, it takes time for buyers to make their buying decision. At these early stages in their product's life, most companies have very limited budgets for hiring salespeople so they are sales-force-limited. Combining these factors, it is very difficult for a company to accurately predict its sales volumes for the first few years.

As a company grows and expands its sales force, it should be able to create a sales productivity model; it should be able, through experience, to learn how long it takes to train a salesperson, how long it takes a new salesperson to become productive, and what volume of sales to expect from a new salesperson. There is often a tremendous variation in the productivity of sales personnel, and one of the more difficult challenges of a startup company is to nurture and support the producers, while weeding out the non-producers.

Given all of these uncertainties, it takes an extremely disciplined approach to create realistic projections for a company's sales in its first few years.

The Difficulty of Estimating Expenses

While it's easy to overestimate or over-forecast a company's product sales, it's just as easy to underestimate the company's expenses. The most obvious reason is that it's difficult to think of everything that has to be done. The company's managers never put too many tasks on the list; they are much more likely to leave out a few that don't occur to them. In addition, tasks tend to be more complicated and take longer than expected. Very few things happen to accelerate task completion. But it seems like an infinite number of things can cause a task to take longer than expected.

It is for all of these reasons that startup companies usually underestimate expenses. Enormous discipline and experience are required to create realistic expense projections.

The Difficulty of Forecasting Profits

Here's a simple example that illustrates how a difference between two numbers can vary significantly when the input numbers change. Assume that revenues are forecast to be $100 million and expenses including manufacturing cost to be $75 million leaving a profit before tax of $25 million dollars. If revenues decrease by 10 percent to $90 million and expenses increase by 10 percent to $82.5 million, the profit decreases from $25 million to $7.5 million. Ten percent variations in revenue and expenses produced a 70 percent decrease in profit.

This simple example illustrates why it is so critically important to forecast revenue and expenses accurately. Shortfalls in revenue, coupled with overages in expenses, can result in wild variations in profit and cash flow. Such a simple miscalculation has caused many startups to burn through their precious capital before achieving significant milestones that would justify a higher valuation for the company. As a consequence, they must go back to investors in a very weak negotiating position, having not accomplished what they said they would.

Burning Through Cash

One of my companies manufactured a power inverter that had the potential to be used in every television set, which was obviously an enormous market. Following the advice of several angel investors and some not-so-experienced venture capitalists, the company initiated strategic partnering discussions with several of the largest TV manufacturers in the world. This strategy certainly had intuitive appeal and it appeared that the potential revenues could be extremely exciting for an otherwise very small startup company.

Unfortunately, there are several challenges for a startup company seeking to partner with a large corporation: Many large corporations are reluctant to deal with startups.

When large corporations enter into discussions with a potential partner, they perform an exhaustive review of the company's financial strength. They look at the company's balance sheet and they try to get assurance that the company is likely to be in business for years into the future. Most startup companies do not have a strong enough balance sheet to satisfy this criterion.

Moreover, large corporations are extremely process-intensive. In selecting their partners, they do extensive due diligence. They may want to see a working prototype of the product, or develop a joint project in order to prove out manufacturing feasibility and costs. These processes almost always take more than a year to complete, and they can easily take two or more years.

In this company's case, the evaluation process stretched out for several years and it depleted the company's resources, putting it out of business. This process was driven mostly by angel and venture capital investors who, in my opinion, should have known better. Sometimes it's better for small companies to deal with Avis rather than Hertz, meaning it can be better to deal with smaller industry players who seek to compete with the leaders rather than with the leaders themselves.

The late Chuck Drexel[1] was the founder of Tylan Corporation and later of DXL, Inc. Tylan Corp. was a very successful manufacturer of mass flow controllers, devices used to control gas flows during the manufacture of semiconductors. After Chuck left Tylan, he formed DXL, where he continued to invent new and more efficient mass flow controllers. Unfortunately, the major buyers of mass flow controllers are large semiconductor capital equipment companies, and they were not eager to deal with a startup company, in spite of Chuck's prior success.

To build a successful company, it is necessary to raise enough capital to achieve the next major milestones and manage the capital effectively so that the company has enough time to raise the next round of financing and begin work on its next set of major milestones. This is a complicated management task, and it is one of the reasons that first-time founders have difficulty—they either don't understand the process, or they don't execute if effectively.

Conclusion

In the long term, the value of a company is determined by its potential for creating positive cash flow. But in the early stages, value is created in small steps, or milestones, like the addition of a team member, the completion of a prototype product, the retention of a first customer. The leader of a startup must find a sequence of value-creation events that will make his company attractive to investors.

If we're going to raise money from investors, we need to understand how the investment industry works. This is the subject of chapter 5: "Startup Capital: Recent History."

Startup Capital: Recent History

"Is it getting harder for startups to raise money?"

—Lisa Calhoun, General Partner, Valor Ventures, Inc.com

Evolution of Capital Markets for Startups

In order to understand today's markets for startup capital, it is important to understand how the markets have evolved.

The chart on the next page titled Evolving Sources of Capital for Startups summarizes the changes that have taken place since the 1980s. These markets are dramatically different today than they were when Steve Jobs founded Apple, Bill Gates founded Microsoft, and Bill Hewlett and David Packard founded Hewlett-Packard.

Today, venture capital funds have become so large that it is difficult for them to invest in startup companies. Angel groups have tried to fill the vacuum, but with limited success. In order to understand how these changes happened, we need to explore some history.

In 1985 a "large" venture-capital partnership managed $100–150 million in a single fund. A venture capital pool of that size could invest $1–3 million in 25 to 35 companies and build a statistically sound investment portfolio. Most deals were syndicated by two or three venture capital funds, so that a company could raise $10–$20 million or more through a sequence of investments, commonly referred to as Series A, Series B, Series C, etc. The top venture capital firms were actively involved in incubating startup

Evolving Sources of Capital for Startups

1985	1990	1995	2000	2005	2010	2015
						Some IPO activity
			Surviving funds make spectacular returns on dot-com deals	IPO market still shut down	Still no serious IPO exit activity	
		Large funds make good returns from IPOs and acquisitions	Dot-come bubble bursts	Large funds manage $500M and up	VC returns depressed	VC returns recover
Large VC fund manages $150M	Large funds able to protect investments		IPO market shuts down again	Few VC startup investments	Dot-com profits fund a few new funds	A few new VC funds do starups
Actively involved with startup companies	No IPO market since 1987	Large funds survive	Angel groups make some startup investments	Difficult to start new funds	Angels lean toward small-cap deals	Angels struggling to exit small deals
Some IPC activity	Small funds get heavily diluted	Small funds go out of business		Angel groups fill vaccum?		

F. Haney, 2016.

companies. They would sometimes provide office space for startup companies and help them write their business plan and assemble their founding team.

The health of the venture capital industry is closely linked to the level of activity in markets for initial public offerings (IPOs). If limited partners and their investment funds are the life blood of a venture capital firm, then "exits," or the return of capital by IPO or acquisition, are their lifeline to profits. Unfortunately, access to the IPO market comes in unpredictable bursts of activity, which usually do not last very long. According to Quandl, a source for financial and economic data, from 1980 to 2015 there were five time periods when the number of IPOs exceeded approximately sixty per year:

- 1983–1984
- 1986–1987
- 1992

- 1994–1995

- 1996–1999

The Quandl study shows that from 1980 to 2015, the IPO market was robust to the extent of producing over sixty IPOs per year for only ten of the thirty-six years. Moreover, there were fewer than sixty IPOs for almost all of the years between 1999 and 2015.[1]

Where Did All the Exits Go?

There was a robust IPO market during the mid-1980s. On October 19, 1987—known as Black Monday—the Dow Jones Industrial Average declined 22.6 percent on one day. This represents the 17th largest dollar loss since that time, but the next largest percentage drop was only 7.87 percent on October 15, 2008. This severe decline pushed all pending IPOs to "the shelf," meaning that they were on hold until better market conditions returned.

Black Monday ushered in a four-year period during which venture capitalists were unable to "exit" from their investments by way of an IPO. But, in order to maintain their ownership positions, they were often required to invest additional capital to keep their companies alive. During this time, the so-called deep pockets venture capital funds were able to continue supporting their companies and protecting their percentage of ownership. But this was often done at the expense of the smaller venture capital funds, which ran out of funds to invest. If a smaller fund was unable to participate in a round of financing, the participating venture capital firms would often purchase shares at a greatly reduced price, which diluted the smaller fund's percentage of ownership.

As a result, a gulf developed between the large funds and the small ones. The rich got richer and the poor got poorer. Because the smaller firms had lackluster investment results, they were unable to raise additional capital and many were forced out of business. In consequence, the venture capital industry is, in my opinion, top heavy. There are a number of extremely large funds with great track records of success. Almost all of the smaller seed capital funds are relatively young and inexperienced.

Where Did All This Money Come From?

When the IPO market recovered in 1991–94, the larger, surviving funds made huge investment returns. According to *Upside* magazine, in 1992, the 3i Ventures California portfolio tied for fourth place in US IPOs, along with Sequoia Capital and U.S. Venture Partners, with eight IPOs apiece.[2]

Funds that invested aggressively during the middle 1990s made extraordinary returns on some dot-com investments that went public in the late 1990s, provided that they cashed out before the dot-com bubble burst in 2000.

Because of their successes, these larger funds were able to raise much larger amounts of capital for their funds. The size of a "large" venture-capital fund went from $100–150 million in the 1980s to $400 million and even $1 billion or more in the 1990s.

During the late 1990s, because the best venture capital funds became so large, it was almost impossible for them to invest in startup companies. The math just doesn't work. If a venture capital company firm is managing $500 million, its average "capital invested per company" will be approximately $10 million. A fund of this size cannot afford to make very many $1–2 million investments. During this period, the focus of venture capital activity shifted to the later stages of Series B or Series C, or later.

This created a significant void, which persists today, for startup investments. Presumably, various angel investment groups tried to fill this void in the late 1990s and early 2000s, but, as we will see, angel groups are not a direct replacement for venture capital firms.

Whoops! The Exits Went Away Again!

After the dot-com bubble burst in 2000, many venture capital firms went through another cycle of exit starvation. Because I had suffered through the four years after 1987's Black Monday, during which there were few IPOs, my instincts are pretty attuned to the issues affecting the IPO market.

Since 2000, IPO activity has been unpredictable, especially for smaller companies. In my opinion, one reason for this change is the passing of the Sarbanes-Oxley Act of 2002, which increased compliance costs for small public companies, because it significantly increased their financial reporting and control obligations. I had a brief exchange about this, on the Coto de Caze golf course in Southern California, with Congressman Michael Oxley, a co-author of the statute, in 2004. He commented, "Fred, the reason the IPO market is so robust is that the act has given people renewed faith in public companies." My rejoinder was, "Congressman, my sources tell me that the IPO market is still holding back, because of the increased cost of taking a small company public." While the number of IPOs in 2004 was greater than in 2003, it was still fewer than two hundred.

There are certainly other factors at play, beyond the Sarbanes-Oxley Act.

When the IPO market is hot, enormous amounts of value can be created by new companies. However, there are often periods of three years or more when the demand for high-tech IPOs is depressed, making it difficult, if not impossible, for investors to obtain a return of capital from their investments.

Shortly after the stock market started to tank in 1999, I attended a quarterly breakfast briefing hosted by Ernst & Young, the accounting firm, at Shutters on the Beach in Santa Monica. Ernst & Young briefed Southern Californian venture capitalists on the state of the venture capital markets. At this meeting, speakers from Ernst & Young asked the attendees to predict when the IPO market would recover. The winner of the poll would receive a nice bottle of wine. Based on my 1987 experience, I picked the longest period that the poll allowed, something like 2008 or 2009. My logic went like this: On Black Monday in 1987, the stock market dropped 22 percent in a single day, and it took the IPO market over four years to recover. In the case of the dot com bubble, the NASDAQ dropped 78 percent from March 2000 to October 2002. I thought the IPO market could be shut down for a very long time. So, I picked the farthest out year in the poll. It was probably 2008. (Read the next section to see how this worked out.)

Again, there was a period of consolidation in the industry with the smaller venture capital funds, which had been born in the late 1990s and early 2000s, often failing because they were unable to exit their portfolio companies at attractive profits. And, once again, the rich got richer, the large funds survived and expanded, and the smaller partnerships were unable to raise new funds.

Will the IPO Market Ever Come Back?

By 2005, the IPO market still had not recovered except for an occasional blockbuster offer. Some of the top IPOs of the 2000s were:

- Petro China, 2000
- CNOOC Limited (China National Offshore Oil Corporation), 2001
- China Life Insurance, 2003
- Google, 2004
- MasterCard, 2006

Three of these companies were Chinese firms. Two were American. This low level of US IPO activity placed a severe strain on the performance of even the best venture capital funds, some of which had difficulty raising additional capital. Some time-tested firms went out of business because they were unable to raise additional funds. In March 2009, IPOScoop.com pointed to a glimmer of recovery in the IPO market for the first time since 2000.[3]

As there was some recovery in the IPO market starting in 2005, I won a very nice bottle of wine because I had predicted that the recovery could be as many as six years after the peak of IPO activity in 1999. By 2012, there had been some mediocre IPO years but none anywhere near the level of 1999. Some analysts, according to an SEC (Securities and Exchange Commission) report, felt that the Sarbanes-Oxley legislation was still weighing on the IPO market.[4]

Today's capital markets for seed and startup investment are not ideal for startup companies. The top-tier venture capital funds that have the most experience in building companies are so large that they cannot afford to make many investments of less than $5 million. Theoretically, the angel groups can fill the void for investments of $500,000 to $2 or $3 million. But the angel groups lean toward simpler products and less capital-intensive companies than traditional venture capitalists. These forces cause startup companies to ask the following questions:

> If I get startup capital from angel investors, will I be able to get the necessary follow-on capital?
>
> Should I consider a more aggressive strategy that would require $5 million or more, so that I can get on the radar screen of the conventional venture capital firms even though I might give up more equity?

Does it Cost Less Today to Start a Company?

Erin Griffith, now a senior writer for Fortune, wrote on the website Pando Daily, "The dramatic drop in the cost of creating a company over the last decade…has had an obvious effect on the venture capital world. Serious venture investment is not required in the earliest stages of a company's life, so angel investors have been getting the best seed deals."[5]

Average startup costs may be lower, but this is primarily because the mix of technologies has changed. The cost of building a semiconductor or chip company has continued to rise as raw material costs and labor costs have increased. But a larger percentage of startup companies now create software or apps, or other internet-related products and services. These companies can sometimes get to a product with less than a few million dollars, significantly less capital than the more traditional electronics, manufacturing, medical device, or biotechnology companies.

Has this trend driven the average startup cost down? Probably. But the traditional high-tech startups, like semiconductors and pharmaceuticals, may cost more because of inflation, increased regulation, and the ever-rising cost of keeping up with Moore's Law, which calls for computing power to double approximately every year.

Are angel investors getting the best seed deals? Not in my opinion. One difficulty with the new class of lower-cost startups is that they offer fewer competitive advantages. It is very difficult to predict which internet company or which app will be successful because so many rely on consumer psychology to attract customers. It may be to the venture capitalists' advantage to let the angels fund these startups and then invest in the survivors at later stages.

At 3i Ventures, we referred to some deals as "Platinum Record Deals." These were usually companies that relied on retail consumers for revenue. The challenge with these companies is that "You know there will be some platinum records, but how do you decide ahead of time which one will make it to the top of the charts?" When consumer psychology is involved in a product's purchasing decision, it is very difficult to forecast sales or get a clear picture of competition.

Are There Any Contrarian Limited Partners?

In the context of stock market investing, a contrarian is an investor who goes against the crowd. Contrarians lean toward selling when everyone else is buying, and vice versa. In my opinion, very few, if any, of the institutions that provide capital to venture capital funds are contrarian. They seem to invest when markets, especially the IPO market, are hot and hold back funds when they are not. This is especially true of banks, which are sometimes a source of capital for venture capital funds. **This makes venture capital markets extremely volatile, which means every startup company needs a survival plan that does not depend on raising venture capital anytime soon.**

The venture capital industry is definitely a boom or bust industry. One reason for this, I believe, is that the limited partners who provide capital to venture capital funds are almost 100 percent momentum players. They tend to pile into venture capital fund investments when the IPO market is producing attractive returns for investors. But when the IPO market is quiet and the stock markets are depressed, their question for venture capitalists seeking funds is, "What exits have you had recently?"

Nowhere is this momentum phenomenon more obvious than with banks that sometimes finance their own internal venture capital funds. The banks often enter at the peak of the market and exit when things are gloomiest. It's very difficult to find any true "contrarian" limited partners. This factor amplifies the ups and downs of the venture capital industry. It rewards the large funds with significant staying power, and it essentially eliminates the newer, smaller venture capital funds that cannot protect their investments when times are tough. Given the vagaries of the IPO and acquisition markets, the chances that a new venture capital fund will have significant exits are very low.

> I chaired the advisory board of Springbank Tech Ventures, a small early-stage venture capital firm founded in 1996 by four general partners in Calgary, Alberta, Canada. All of the partners had entrepreneurial and managerial backgrounds, which made them an ideal team for providing capital and support to nearby startup companies. Unfortunately for Springbank, their investments matured and began seeking exit opportunities during the 2000s, when there were very few IPOs or acquisitions.
>
> As a result, Springbank was unable to raise a second fund. Unfortunately, in my opinion, they were victims of the "momentum" thinking of limited partners.
>
> To highlight the point, in 2010, I received a "carried interest" check for an investment that my 3i Ventures team made in 1988—twenty-two years earlier. This was unusual, but it does illustrate that companies often take much longer than expected to get to an exit. In my opinion, the venture capital industry needs more limited partners that understand that VCs have little control over the exit timing for their portfolio companies.

So, Who's Doing Startups?

Speaking of a startup in the traditional sense, the answer is almost no one, but none of the VCs or angels would admit this.

The venture capitalists will say they do startups, but it's difficult for most of them to make investments smaller than $5 million. Most of their investments are in later stage companies or the more capital intensive startups, which require more than $5 million to launch. It may make sense for them to invest smaller amounts, if they can be assured of putting more money to work in the same company at a later stage. A large venture capital firm might invest in Series A, provided that they receive the right to invest in Series B and Series C.

The angels and angel groups will say they do startups, and they do, but they often lean toward less complex, less disruptive (as defined and discussed in chapter 1: Introduction), and less capital-intensive investments—not necessarily the kind of startups that the venture capitalists were funding in the 1980s.

Given the shape of today's capital markets, many startup companies are in no man's land. Their initial capital needs are too small to attract venture capitalists, and their businesses are too capital intensive, disruptive, and complex to appeal to most angels. The answer is often to approach both venture capitalists and angel groups, but the company's business plan needs to be customized to the interests of each investor audience.

How Much Venture Capital Is Invested Each Year in the United States?

The PricewaterhouseCoopers MoneyTree survey is a periodic survey of venture capital activity in the United States. The data for Q3 2016 shows that the total amount of capital invested by venture capital firms grew fairly steadily from roughly $8 billion in 1995 to over $40 billion in 2015-2016.[6] This is a cumulative growth rate of approximately 8 percent per year. The growth is punctuated, however by two periods of greatly accelerated activity: the blowout that created the dot-com bubble in 1999-2001 and a more recent bubble that started in 2014. Startup investments are a relatively small percentage of venture capital activity, but there is almost always money available for quality ideas.

Crowdfunding: A New Path to Capital?

In the past few years, a new source of capital known as "crowdfunding" has gained popularity. In crowdfunding, capital is raised over the internet in small amounts, but from a large number of investors. Crowdfunding is an online variation of the angel group concept. It permits a startup company to raise meaningful amounts of capital in very small "bites" from a large number of people.

Kickstarter is perhaps the most well-known crowdfunding website. According to Kickstarter's website, it helps artists, musicians, filmmakers, designers, and other creators find the resources and support they need to make their ideas a reality.[7] An example of a successful Kickstarter campaign for a startup is the Jubilee, a small, metallic, decorative tree. At last count, 126 people made advance payments totaling $23,000 to help pay for its initial inventory.

Crowdfunds are solicited online. Sometimes contributors, which we can think of as investors, receive a gift or product in exchange for their "investment." More recently, though, the concept has expanded to permit equity investing, in which investors review business plans online, and they have the option of purchasing stock in the offering company. Amounts are limited to $1 million per company per year.

What problem does crowdfunding solve? Let's look at some cases: If a company has a less-than blockbuster business concept, it might be able to raise capital through crowdfunding where it could not raise capital from venture capitalists or angels. But this is likely to be a dead-end street unless the company raises all the capital it will ever need.

The same would be true of a company with a blockbuster idea but a nonfundable management team. Such a company might get capital from crowdfunding but it is unlikely to raise additional capital from angels or venture capitalists.

The company most likely to benefit from crowdfunding is one with both a fundable idea and a fundable management team. If the company can raise enough capital through crowdfunding to meet major milestones, then it may be able to raise angel or venture capital at a higher valuation than would otherwise have been possible.

Crowdfunders ("man in the street investors") are at a significant disadvantage compared to professional investors. Many will not be able to build sufficiently diversified portfolios in order to manage the risk of investing in startup companies. Most will not have the sophistication to perform proper due diligence or to know the value of the companies they are investing in. They will be at the mercy of the website sponsors and the companies presenting their information.

Only time will tell us if crowdfunding will develop into a serious source of capital for deserving companies, or if it will simply provide an interesting hobby for people who are fascinated by new technologies and product ideas. Time will tell us if crowdfunding investors will be adequately protected against the risks of investing in startup companies.

While it may be tempting to take advantage of crowdfunding, most high-tech companies with truly promising concepts and strong management teams will still eventually need the larger amounts of capital provided by venture capital financing, so a key to the success of crowdfunding will be the investors' ability to select companies that will be able to attract venture capital for their future growth.

Conclusion

In today's investment markets, there is no single obvious and compelling source of capital for startup companies. Angel investors may be a source for smaller amounts of startup capital. Venture capitalists may be a source for larger amounts. A startup company has to explore all of its options. It must have a range of financing strategies and pursue all options until something works.

In chapter 6: "Venture Capital Think," we will learn how venture capitalists think about the investments they make.

CHAPTER 6

Venture Capital Think

"You know what works in venture capital? A group of incredibly smart, connected people who have the financial where-
withal and risk appetite to make multi-million dollar bets on
unproven ideas and inexperienced founders. People who can
make decisions quickly, and who spend their time trying to
help entrepreneurs make the most of that cash."

—Sarah Lacy, Inc.com

If a company is going to raise money from venture capitalists, it
needs to know how venture capitalists view the world of startup
companies. This chapter is an overview of

Who the venture capitalists are

How they think about their business

Chapters 7 and 8 offer more detail about specific criteria that
a company must satisfy to get the attention of a venture capitalist.

Who Are the VCs and How Do They Think?

Sarah Lacy concisely captures what venture capitalists do. I might
quarrel a little with her reference to "inexperienced founders,"
because I believe venture capitalists actually make every effort to
work with experienced founders. But her basic idea is correct.

VC investors are professional investors who are usually managing other people's money. Most venture capital firms are partnerships headed by a relatively small number of general partners. They obtain capital commitments from limited partners, who are usually institutional investors, corporations, banks, or very high-net-worth individual investors. They try to invest the funds over a period of about four years, and they hope to provide profits from the investments to their limited partners over a period of ten years from the initiation of the fund, although this time limitation is often extended, because companies can take longer than expected to return investors' capital by achieving an "exit."

The Structure of Venture Capital Partnerships

Venture capital firms come in different shapes and sizes. The generic model consists of:

- General or managing partners
- An operating agreement
- Limited partners

General or managing partners are the individuals who will make investment decisions, manage all operational aspects of the partnership, create a portfolio of investments, sit on boards of directors of portfolio companies, and generally manage the partnership's investment activity.

It is customary for the general partners to draw approximately 2.5 percent of the fund's total capital to pay for their annual operating expenses. Over the normal ten-year lifetime of a fund, this represents 25 percent of the capital committed to the fund by the general partners. This percentage might be more for a smaller fund, and less for a larger fund.

The general partners usually receive a carried interest—a percentage of the fund's net profit. This percentage is usually between

15–25 percent, and payments to the managing partners are subject to various restrictions so that they receive a share of the profit only if the fund is truly successful.

The limited partners are the providers of capital to the venture capital fund. Usually the limited partners' capital is not provided all at once. Rather, it is "drawn down," either periodically or as needed by the managing partners.

Most venture capital partnerships are small when first formed. It is common for new partnerships to include fewer than five managing partners. If the fund is successful, it may add managing partners, but only the largest partnerships have more than 10 managing partners.

The task of the managing partners is to:

- Market the fund (find the capital to be invested).

- Identify attractive investment opportunities.

- Negotiate investments.

- Syndicate investments with other venture capitalists.

- Create a risk management portfolio.

- Monitor the progress of portfolio companies.

- Sit on the boards of directors of portfolio companies.

- Help portfolio companies succeed.

- Help with the exit of portfolio companies by IPO or acquisition.

The general partners are highly incentivized to make wise investment decisions, which means managing risk effectively. Included in their toolbox for managing risk are detailed competitive analysis, careful market analysis, carefully fact-checking of information provided by the company, and meticulous vetting of CEOs and management teams.

Where Do Venture Capitalists Come From?

There is no well-defined path to becoming a venture capitalist. If an individual is desperate to become a venture capitalist, his best option is probably to find one or two partners and try to raise capital for a new fund from a few high-net-worth individuals. Existing partnerships add additional partners only as necessary and often at a lower carried interest level.

Another path to becoming a venture capitalist involves starting as an intern or associate for an existing venture capital partnership and working one's way up through the ranks to general partner. In my experience, however, this has not been a very fruitful path for most who have tried it. Associates often work for five years or more only to discover that there is no easy path to becoming a managing partner. The carried interest in a venture capital partnership is very closely guarded.

Some venture capitalists pursued a financial career path to their position. They started in banking or investment banking and they were able to export their skills to a venture capital firm.

Many of the top venture-capital firms reach out to highly successful CEOs or entrepreneurs when they want to expand their team. These venture capital firms know that their business is about building successful companies, so they augment their staffs with people who have been successful in building companies.

One of the reasons that 3i Ventures outperformed about 75 percent of other venture capital funds in its "class" (year of formation) is that I hired investment executives who had held CEO-level positions earlier in their careers. All had senior executive experience and a great deal of knowledge about what is involved in building a successful high-tech company.

Time management challenges practically define a VC. It is critical for a venture capitalist to manage his time efficiently. A venture capitalist usually has dozens of business plans on his desk waiting to be read. He has dozens of people seeking to get on his calendar. He probably sits on ten or more boards of directors, each of which occupies half a day or more per month on his calendar. In order to manage their time effectively, venture capitalists learn that if they are going to say no, they must do so quickly. They ask themselves, "What are the potentially fatal problems with this company? If this company is going to fail, what would cause it to fail? Can the issues be resolved or fixed? Can I get comfortable with the risk they represent? Or should I just say no now?" This approach may make the VCs appear negative, but the focus on these kinds of issues is simply a matter of time management for an investor.

Reliance on Management

The strongest and most disruptive idea is useless unless the startup company has a management team that can turn the idea into a cost-effective product and market it successfully. From a venture capitalist's point of view, the team must have skilled individuals in each role, and the members must be able to work together effectively under the leadership of the CEO.

A venture capitalist's interface with a portfolio company is almost exclusively through the CEO. The CEO is the primary source of information, and she is the most important agent for influencing the direction of the company. A venture capitalist cannot interact significantly below the level of the CEO without creating conflict within the management team. VCs are very aware that they need to invest in companies with CEOs that they can work with, which implies that those CEOs must have good executive and communication skills and an honest, straightforward approach to discussing problems and issues.

Venture capitalists try to invest in CEOs that have proven executive skills and prior successes—preferably in the same field as the company they are running. They also prefer CEOs who have successfully managed venture-capital-backed companies. Venture capitalists usually do extensive reference checking before they invest in executives. The best references are positive ones from venture capitalists that the CEO has worked with in the past.

In selecting a CEO, a venture capitalist looks first for experience. He has seen successful companies created by experienced CEOs, and most have also seen first-time CEOs fail at trying to build a company.

But sometimes a VC has to compromise high standards. Not all CEOs have previous successes, much less with a VC-backed company in the same industry. A venture capital investor might be willing, for example, to invest in a CEO who has previous success as a general manager or a C-level executive within a larger company, that is, a "chief" office such as a chief financial (CFO) or chief technology officer (CTO). It helps if the CEO can state clearly that she implemented successful growth strategies for the managed companies. In any case, the CEO must have strong and demonstrated executive and company-building skills.

A CEO does not always get the job done. In my own 3i Ventures portfolio of twelve companies, six first-time CEOs needed to be replaced, each one for different reasons. One technical founder had almost no management skills. Another first-time CEO was not able to put together the all-important strategic relationships the company needed. Another had some management experience, but he was unable to meet the simplest targets set by his board of directors. Another did a poor job of managing the company's cash; he almost spent the company into insolvency.

In each case, I approached the board of directors and initiated a discussion about the performance of the CEO.

Over a period of months, the boards decided to make a CEO change. Not all of the replacement CEOs were successful, but it was clear that previous C-level executive experience can improve the likelihood of success for a CEO.

When a corporation is initially formed, the officers and board of directors are often friends and colleagues of the founder. But when venture capitalists invest, they will almost certainly want representation on the board of directors, and, in many cases, they will want management and investors to be represented equally, with a mutually agreed-upon "tiebreaker" member of the board. Part of a venture capitalist's decision to invest, or not, is based on his opinion of the members of the board of directors and how easy they will be to work with.

Managing Risk

Venture capitalists play a risky game by investing in early-stage high-tech startup companies. They control risk by building portfolios of thirty or more investments and by being extremely selective in their investment choices. They perform extensive due diligence on all aspects of a company, including the CEO's past executive experience. They are under intense pressure to put their limited partners money to work, but they also must balance the risk they take against the potential rewards.

VC investors are always looking for attractive investment opportunities, but they are extremely cautious about accepting known risks. They perceive risks of several types:

- Technical risk—does the technology work?
- Development risk—can the product be built?

- Market acceptance risk—will customers buy the product?

- Execution risk—can the management team make it happen?

- Financial risk—will the company raise enough money to be successful?

Generally, they prefer investments that involve only one or two of the major risk categories. Most companies present some form of market acceptance risk, execution risk, and financial risk. Therefore, it is extremely important to eliminate technical risk and development risk, if at all possible. This is a powerful argument for pursuing a survival, or bootstrapping, strategy.

Execution risk involves the collective risk that the management team, under the leadership of the CEO, will be able to achieve the company's objectives on schedule and within budget. Venture capitalists have learned that the success of a management team is critically dependent on the skills of the CEO.

A VC's CEO Detector

Do VCs need a sixth sense for selecting the "most likely to succeed" CEOs and management teams? Not really. It's often easier than you might think for a VC to distinguish an inexperienced CEO from an experienced one. Inexperienced CEOs telegraph their inexperience in many ways.

Many inexperienced, first-time founders or CEOs would be shocked and surprised if they realized how easily a VC can tell that they are novices. They might as well wear a tee shirt that says "First-time CEO." Why? Because the inexperienced founder says things that an experienced CEO would never say. Here are some examples:

We have no competition.

A venture capitalist understands that this claim is rarely true. All companies have competition. Assuming that the company's product solves some problem, there are probably other ways of solving the problem. Each of these other solutions is a form of competition for the startup. Another vendor's product does not have to use the same methods or technologies to be a competitive product. For example, Amazon's competition is not just other online retailers. They must also compete with retailers that have stores that appeal to consumers who like the touch and feel aspects of shopping. When a VC hears, "We have no competition," what he really hears is, "We don't really know how to assess the competition in our industry." A careful assessment of that competition almost always results in an array of buyers, suppliers, existing vendors, and substitute products (alternative solutions to the problem) that define the competitive space within which a company must operate.

We only need 1 percent of an enormous market.

It is clear that the founder who says this does not understand how markets are segmented and that a company's profitability often depends on having significant market share within their served market (the market we really intend to address)—preferably in excess of 20 percent. What the venture capitalist hears is, "We don't really understand how to segment our market or how to define our served market, and we certainly don't understand that companies with significant market share are more likely to be profitable and successful."

Our product is better than anything out there.

Almost every company can make this claim. But the venture capitalist hears "We don't really know how to define 'better' in our industry, and we don't really know how much better a product would have to be to get customers excited." The important question is not is it better, but rather what do we mean by better? How much better is the product? Is it better enough to compel customers to buy it?

Our technology speaks for itself.

This is one of the most common miscalculations that inventor-founders make. In their own mind's eye, they have made an exquisite invention. They have solved one of the world's most difficult problems and the value of their invention should be obvious to all.

The problem, of course, is that the inventor has substantially more context and understanding than the rest of us have. She may have worked for years in the field and may have a unique understanding of existing solutions and their shortcomings. She may have an advanced degree in biochemistry or physics and, therefore, may understand elements of science that are a mystery to most people. She may have invented a device or system that is so incredibly complex that few people can understand it.

For many inventions, it may be very difficult for the layperson to understand the technology. The difficulty is not just that the invention is complicated. The inventor assumes that the invention can be easily understood, and that its value is obvious to all. Therefore she never learns to describe it in language that can be easily understood by all.

Our management team has extensive industry contacts.

There is nothing wrong with having extensive contacts. The issue is that some companies have expectations for their contacts or the contacts of others that are simply not realistic. For a variety of reasons, the value of contacts decays rapidly. People change jobs within companies, people change companies, people move to different responsibilities, people move to other parts of the world. It is a great advantage to have valuable contacts, but it is a mistake to rely heavily on them.

Strong leaders know that if they need access to a particular company or person they can find a way to get an introduction. This is important. A company's ability to create contacts is more important than its present collection of contacts.

Our CEO has extensive management experience.

Venture capitalist hear this as shorthand for "our CEO has never been a CEO before." He may have managed a sales organization, or an engineering department, but that experience does not necessarily qualify him to be an effective startup company CEO.

We have important strategic partnerships.

In response to this claim, an experienced venture capitalist asks "Do you have anything in writing?" Typically, conversations are preliminary and nothing has been agreed upon contractually. A seasoned CEO would make that distinction by either saying "we are in preliminary discussions," or "we have a signed contract with ABC Corp."

We will be cash-flow positive in less than one year.

This would be great if it really happened. Unfortunately, it rarely does. Most startup companies raise barely enough capital to operate for 12 to 18 months. During that time, they are usually introducing a new product to market, and sales are likely to be modest.

After the initial product launch, additional investment is usually required to cover losses as the company expands its manufacturing, marketing, and sales operations. So, in a traditional world, it is highly unlikely that a company will become cash positive in less than one year. This claim is usually a signal that the company has overestimated revenues or underestimated costs. The exception in today's market might be an application, software, or internet company that is able to generate income with very little expense.

The venture capitalist hears "we don't really know how to forecast our profit margins. We just want to put in big numbers to impress you." What the inexperienced founder doesn't know is that most venture capitalists have heard this hundreds of times but they've probably never seen it happen. Most high-tech companies need $5 million or more to become cash positive. What the investor hears is "we don't really know how to estimate our revenues, profit margins, and operating expenses in order to create a plausible cash flow projection."

Some internet and application companies have managed to achieve stellar levels of revenue and profits with very little capital investment. These companies present a different kind of challenge to venture capitalists, who must determine which ones will be successful. When the outcome depends heavily on consumer psychology, it's very difficult to predict which will succeed. We deal with this issue in more detail in chapter 7.

Our new "engine design" will revolutionize Detroit.

This statement represents different approaches that have one thing in common: they fight City Hall. There's nothing wrong with revolutionizing Detroit or energy production, or water desalinization, or the way municipal police departments operate. The problem for most venture capitalist is that they know that these kinds of businesses generally take years of frustrating lobbying and campaigning with large bureaucracies before the first sale is made. Automobile engines, for example, are designed years in advance. So it's very difficult for a company to have significant impact in fewer than about 10 years. Which is well beyond the time horizon in which a venture capitalist expects to exit from his investment.

Our forecast is very conservative.

This can be a two-edged sword. Venture capitalists don't necessarily want to see conservative forecasts; they want to see achievable and realistic forecasts. The ultimate test for a venture capitalist, then, is not whether the forecast is conservative. The test is the following:

> Is the forecast believable?
>
> is it defensible?
>
> Is it achievable?

Startup company founders often feel a conflict between producing a conservative forecast and an aggressive forecast. They shouldn't do either. They should focus on producing the most believable and defensible forecast possible. What is the most realistic forecast that they can defend? These are the more important questions.

Our company's valuation will yield an attractive return on investment for our investors.

It is acceptable to say this, but more experienced CEOs leave the valuation issues to the venture capitalists. After all, valuation and return on investment are precisely the bailiwick of venture capital investors. So why try to do their job for them? Besides, any return on investment calculation that a founder makes is likely to be wrong in the eyes of a professional investor, so why take the chance?

We plan to go public in three to five years.

The problem with this statement is that it reveals a lack of understanding of the unpredictable and cyclical nature of public markets.

During the past 30 years there have been periods of 4 (1987–1990) and 10 (2000–2009) years when initial public offerings were not available to most early stage companies. IPO markets are so volatile that it's difficult to say there is business as usual. In fact, business as usual implies relatively scattered, random, and short windows of opportunity during which companies can go public. But the windows are impossible to predict. They depend on economic conditions, stock market behavior, the regulatory environment, and other factors that cannot be controlled.

We have a luminary group of industry expert advisers.

It's great to have knowledgeable advisers. However, venture capitalists are usually skeptical when they see a long list of highly successful individuals listed as advisers for a startup. Such a list provokes these questions:

- How involved are these people, really?
- How often do they meet?
- How much of their time do they give you?
- If these successful guys are part of your team, why do you need money from me?

It is best to position advisers as accurately as possible. For example, say "These individuals spend half a day per month with us, and they have helped us in the following ways." And then be specific.

Any forecast we come up with will be wrong.

A statement like this reveals the CEO is probably very naïve about business planning processes. Forecasts are not expected to be accurate. No one can predict the future. A forecast is not a prediction. It is a reasoned argument in support of a plausible future revenue and profit stream. The questions are: is it reasonable, believable, logical, and defensible? And can it be supported?

Revenues will quadruple but expenses will remain the same.

Forecasts like this usually reveal that the presenter does not have a good understanding of business finance. Some business costs are fixed, such as headquarters and corporate administrative costs. Some, such as manufacturing, sales and marketing, service, and installation vary with the amount of product manufactured and sold. Usually, when revenues increase, the variable costs increase as well, because more product must be manufactured, more marketing and sales resources are required, and more service and installation people are needed. When a company projects substantial increases in revenue without corresponding increases in variable costs, it is usually underestimating the increased sales and marketing resources that will be required to obtain the additional revenue. An exception occurs if the company makes significant improvements in sales productivity. As sales people mature and learn more about selling a product, their productivity can increase significantly. This can lead to increased sales without corresponding increases in sales and marketing costs. A company needs to explain exactly what assumptions it is making about its sales productivity and how the increases are being obtained.

Putting It Together

Each of the statements above illustrates a difference between a first-time management team and an experienced one. The differences are significant, and they are readily apparent to an experienced investor, who has probably dealt with both. Most venture capitalists have learned that experienced managers do a better job of grappling with the difficult issues of building a company.

Years ago, just for fun, I created a presentation called "The Many Hats a VC Wears" to make the point that a venture capitalist has to have a very broad range of skills. I put on a collection of different hats, each with a humorous venture capital interpretation.

The green eyeshade, of course, symbolizes the financial analysis and company valuation modeling that a venture capitalist must do.

The magician's hat stands for the fact that a venture capitalist has to pull a rabbit out of the hat once in a while in order to have a profitable portfolio.

The cone-shaped wizard's hat, covered with astrological symbols, helps a VC pull off the occasional mandatory magic trick.

There is also a mystical swami hat that comes with a crystal ball that utters such helpful phrases as, "You've got me there," and "Say that again!"

The bullfighter's hat illustrates the need for occasional jousting with company managers, other venture capitalists, and strategic partners.

The contractor's hard hat is protection against the onslaught of companies trying to get into a VC's office and constantly hassling the venture capitalist in order to get on his calendar.

The golf cap is useful for the occasional business golf outing.

The cowboy hat is a reminder that the frontiers of technology are often like the frontiers of the wild, wild west.

The mad hatter's hat is for the venture capitalist to give to his partners when they've done something especially goofy.

The top hat is for formal occasions when the venture capitalist is invited to serve on committees for charitable fundraiser events.

The yachtsmen's hat is reserved for the venture capitalist's retirement plan, assuming things have gone well and he is able to purchase a wildly expensive yacht.

The hats are entertaining and fun, but they make a very important point. The best venture capitalists are talented multidisciplinary professionals, who are usually very astute in their assessment of products and management teams. It takes a high-quality proposition to get their attention, but it can be done.

Do Venture Capitalists Invest in Ideas, or in People?

What do venture capitalists actually invest in: ideas or people? You would think the answer would always be both, but it isn't. Some investors say they invest in people, because if they invest in "the best people," they will always come up with the "best ideas." I had this conversation several times over dinner with Jean DeLeage, of the VC firm Burr, Egan, Deleage & Co. He argued strenuously that he invested in people who would come up with the best ideas.

In my experience, invention and creativity are not systematic, repeatable processes. Not many people can invent on demand. Further, the people who come up with the best ideas are not necessarily the people who will be able to manage a company to success.

In my view, someone who claims to invest only in people is usually exaggerating. I don't believe anyone invests in *just* people or *just* ideas. It takes both to make a successful startup business. But an investor can certainly focus on one over the other. Would anyone invest in a top-notch CEO with a bad idea? I doubt it.

Presumably, a really bad idea will always be a bad idea and no amount of exceptional execution will fix it.

So, let's assume that our people-oriented investor does find good people who come up with good ideas. There's nothing wrong with that. Good people and good ideas are a winning combination every time. But let's examine the premise. Is the process of identifying good people feasible? How can we identify outstanding executives who can come up with good ideas? How do we know when we've found one? We can check references to see if our executive has strong management skills. But how do we convince ourselves that she can invent a blockbuster product when tasked to do so?

Where do good ideas come from? In my opinion, very few brilliant business ideas come from experienced executives. Most seem to come from people who:

- Work in the trenches.
- Work in laboratories.
- Work with products.
- Make things and see a better way.
- See the shortcomings of current methods.

If I were forced to choose between a good idea and a good executive, I would always choose the good idea. If it's truly a blockbuster idea, I have an excellent chance of recruiting capable management to implement it. But if I instead choose the good executive, I could wait a lifetime for him to come up with a truly good idea. If I go for the good idea, at least I have a chance of building a successful company. I have some control over my destiny.

Warren Buffett may have said it best: "When a management with a reputation for brilliance tackles a business with a reputation for bad economics, it is the reputation of the business that remains intact."[1]

Remember, though, that time management is extremely important to a venture capitalist. The bottom line is as long as a venture capitalist sees investment opportunities with both a good idea and good management, he will focus on those because they represent the shortest path to a deal.

Do VCs Recruit Management Teams for Companies They Like?

If venture capitalists believe that it is essential to have experienced CEOs and managers in their portfolio companies, why don't they just invest in companies with blockbuster ideas and recruit a management team they like? Here are three possible reasons:

- It takes too much time, and it basically puts a venture capitalist into the executive recruiting business, which is not what they are paid to do. Venture capitalists don't generally have to recruit management teams, because they see enough deals with experienced and qualified management teams.

- Sometimes venture capitalists do bring in management. If a venture capitalist sees a company whose people are pitching an especially good idea, he may decide to invest the time and energy needed to recruit a qualified CEO and to build a strong management team. For example, 3i Ventures helped to write the business plan for Gensia Pharmaceuticals, and it helped recruit David Hale, an experienced CEO, in order to assure the company's ability to attract capital.

- Venture capital firms sometimes have a temporary relationship with an executive that is referred to as an executive in residence, or a CEO in residence. These experienced executives are usually CEOs with whom the venture capital firm has had a good experience in the past. The executive in residence helps the venture capital firm evaluate deals until he sees one that appears to be promising. Then, the venture capital firm might decide to make an investment in the company on the condition that their executive in residence becomes the full-time CEO.

The operative assumption should be that venture capitalists are not in the management-finding business, however, there are exceptions. Let's look at an example.

Example of a Venture Capitalist Recruiting a CEO

A well-known venture capitalist, Don Valentine of Sequoia Capital, installed a CEO at Cisco Systems as a condition for investing—with an extremely positive outcome. Here's a summary from *The History of Cisco*, by George Garza:

> The early days were difficult; at times making payroll was a challenge. It was not until 1988 that Donald Valentine was approached that things changed. Valentine was a venture capitalist and agreed to capitalize Cisco Systems. In return he would be given stock ownership control of the company. This meant that the old management team was replaced. First he brought in John Morgridge as president and CEO. Over the next few years, while the internet grew, the demand for networking devices also grew. Cisco was, as they say, in the right place at the right time.[2]

Prior to Cisco, Morgridge was president and COO of GRiD Systems, and before that he held senior positions with Stratus Computer and Honeywell Information.[3]

Conclusion

What kind of idea or business concept excites a venture capitalist? It is not surprising that most of them are looking for extremely "big" ideas with enormous commercial potential. A VC firm needs a few big winners in every portfolio to make its overall returns "pencil out" or make financial sense.

In chapter 7: "The Fundable Idea," we'll see how they think about big ideas.

CHAPTER 7

The Fundable Idea

"Disrupt or be disrupted. There is no middle ground."

—Jay Samit, *Disrupt You!*

What kind of business concept or idea does it take to get the attention of a venture capitalist? How good does an idea have to be? How is good defined? It's very important that the leader of a startup company know which ideas might be fundable by venture capitalists and which probably will not be. A good place to start is by explaining what makes an idea disruptive.

What Is a Disruptive Idea?

Venture capital investors want to fund products that solve important problems. Presumably, if a product solves an important problem, there should be lots of demand for the product and it should have the potential to produce significant revenue. VCs usually decline to invest if a company cannot plausibly demonstrate that it has the potential to earn at least $50 to $100 million in sales within about five years. In the pharmaceutical industries, the target for annual sales is often $1 billion, because a primary path for exit from an investment is the sale of the company to a large pharmaceutical company. Most "pharma" companies are so large that it makes little sense for them to acquire businesses that do not have the potential for $1 billion per year, or more, in annual revenue, but it can take ten years or more to achieve this level.

A disruptive idea has the potential to change the world. A disruptive product makes dramatic changes in the way a problem is solved. It stands the world on its head. A venture capitalist is interested in *better* products but defines better as "*substantially* better than anything that exists today." This means *measurably* better than existing products and solutions using credible metrics.

Some examples of inventions that changed our lives in significant ways are:

- Telephone answering machine
- Word processor
- Internet
- Artificial Intelligence
- E-mail
- Bluetooth
- DVR (Digital Video Recorder)
- Smart phone
- Ultrasound imaging
- Digital photography

Not all disruptive inventions will have such broad application, but this is the kind of impact investors are seeking.

What Does It Mean to Solve an Important Problem?

After managing 3i Ventures for several years, I realized that there was an interesting distinction between our biotech investments and our traditional technology and computer-related investments. Most of the biotech companies were trying to solve important problems, such as developing a cure for cancer or some other serious disease, for example. Determining the size of the market is often as simple as how many people suffer from the disease—usually a large number. For the biotech companies, the key questions of due diligence are:

> Can the team develop the solution?
>
> Will the technology work?
>
> Can the technology be used to develop a cost effective product?

In contrast to biotech, many of the traditional technology products were created by inventors who did not know what problem their product would solve. In these cases, the important questions were:

> Does the product solve an important problem?
>
> Is someone lying awake at night wishing they had this product?
>
> What problem or problems can the solution solve?
>
> How many people have this problem?
>
> Will the solution be compelling enough to motivate customers to buy the product?

Whether a company starts with the solution or the problem, the challenge is the same: In order to attract investors, it must convince them that its technology or its product solves an important problem.

The emphasis on companies with big and disruptive ideas is a critical aspect of a venture capital firm's portfolio strategy. Studies have shown that a venture capital firm needs a portfolio of thirty to thirty-five companies to have a reasonable chance of being successful. Out of sixty companies in the 3i Ventures portfolio, nineteen became public companies, about one-third were acquired, and about one-third failed. This is better than average, but it helps to illustrate the point that a few companies with exceptional returns are required to make a portfolio successful. In our case, we didn't have any spectacular (100X or 1,000X, meaning one hundred times our investment, or one thousand times our investment) returns, but we did have enough 10–20X returns to produce an overall return in the top quartile for funds in our class.

Venture capitalists look for companies with both disruptive products and these attributes:

- A sustainable competitive advantage
- Patents to protect their product positioning
- Sufficient market opportunity to build a business with $100 million, or more, in annual revenues
- A realistic, achievable business plan
- A viable business model, or plan for obtaining revenues, profits, and a respectable return on investment
- An initial valuation that will permit the venture capital firm to make an attractive profit

Let's look at each of these attributes.

A Sustainable Competitive Advantage

A compelling startup company will have a clearly stated competitive positioning target and a strategy for achieving it. That is, ways of measuring "better" and achieving competitive advantage over existing products. But simple competitive advantage is not sufficient. It does no good for a company to have competitive advantage today if it won't have competitive advantage in five years. Venture capital investors look for companies that can have competitive advantage that will be sustained over an extended period of time. Venture capital investments are usually predicated on an "unfair and sustainable competitive advantage."

"Unfair" in this context simply means that the advantage is substantial and difficult to overcome, like a basketball player who is six inches taller, or a wrestler who weights 25 pounds more. VCs know that if a company has a significant, lasting advantage over its competition, the likelihood that they will achieve an attractive return on investment is greater than if it does not have that advantage. If a company's eventual acquirers will require a sustainable advantage of five to ten years, then the initial investors will need a competitive horizon of ten to twenty years, since it usually takes companies five to ten years to achieve an exit.

Competitive advantage means that a company's product has specific, measurable benefits that make it more attractive to buyers than other products. But, especially in high-tech markets, it is easier for small companies to capitalize on new science and technology first because they can move faster. But when the larger companies do enter the market, they have more mass and more investment capital and often end up winning competitive battles. Hence, venture capital investors want companies that have *sustainable* competitive advantage, which means that they have enough advantage to stay on top over a period of five or ten years or longer.

Recently, I met with a company that describes itself as a smart phone marketing company. In reviewing their business plan presentation, I noticed that they claimed to have no competition. So, as a quick sanity check, I did a Google search using the phrase "smart phone marketing company." By putting the phrase "smart phone marketing company" in quotes, I assured that I would only receive responses from websites that specifically use the complete phrase "smart phone marketing company." I received 62,500 responses to the search. Did that tell me that there are 62,500 smart phone marketing companies? Of course not. But the search certainly suggested that there were likely to be at least some other smart phone marketing companies. To continue my due diligence process, I would need to look at some of the listings and see if they were in fact smart phone marketing companies. Venture capitalists often ask one of their staff to do a quick test like this to see if it confirms a company's claims.

Patents to Protect Products

Proprietary technology is usually protected by one or more patents. While not all patents offer strong protection against competition, some do. Part of the venture capitalist's challenge is to figure out how protective a particular patent, or family of patents, is likely to be.

Patents are complicated, difficult to read, and written in language that not everyone can understand. Some patents are broader than others. For example, the GORE-TEX® patents have provided extensive protection for a particular type of fabric for the lifetime of the patent. However, some method and systems patents protect a particular way of solving a problem but might not protect against a slightly different way of solving the same problem. Venture capitalists need to know exactly what competitive protection is provided by a patent and exactly what the patent would prohibit competitors from doing.

A Realistic and Achievable Business Plan

Too many business plans are riddled with words like better, faster, cheaper, smaller, bigger, and various unsubstantiated claims. Venture capitalists look for business plans that contain specific goals and objectives that they confidently believe can be achieved. Specificity, realism, and achievability are critical. There should be no unjustified claims.

A Viable Business Model

A company's business model is its plan for producing revenues and profits, presumably in enough volume to provide an attractive return on investment. Not all businesses "pencil out." Markets may be too small. Prices may be too low. Costs may be too high. Investment requirements may be excessive. A good business plan explains the business model and why it will work.

Achieving a Good Initial Valuation

Venture capitalists invest in companies at valuations that give them a reasonable chance to make a good return on investment. They use a company's business plan forecasts to estimate exit valuations and possible investment returns. Usually, the two parties are able to negotiate a valuation that is mutually acceptable. Relatively few deals blow up because founders insist on too high a valuation, but it does happen. How can a startup protect itself against too low a valuation? The best defense is a good NPV model, a spread sheet that projects the company's future cash flows and calculates their net present value. If a startup has its own NPV model, the value negotiation is more likely to become a discussion about the assumptions underlying the forecast and less likely to be a push and shove kind of negotiation.

Where Do Good Ideas Come From?

The creative process is mysterious. No one knows exactly how it works. For the more than one hundred companies I have dealt with, the ideas originated primarily in the laboratory or in the market. Almost all of the successful companies were a partnership between a smart inventor and an executive with a proven track record.

Here is a partial list of the origins of some of the big ideas I have been involved with:

- Improvement of an existing technology.

- Use of an existing technology to solve a different problem.

- Combining existing businesses to form a more competitive business.

- Using a new technology to solve a known problem.

- Combining two technologies in a creative way to get "1 + 1 = 3."

- Expanding on a scientific theory or observation.

- Implementing a better business model in order to gain competitive advantage.

An important caveat: Timing is everything. A startup can fail because its idea is ahead of its time. Speech Systems, the voice recognition software company that was mentioned earlier, is an example. It was probably 20–25 years ahead of its time in the sense that the early technology was too expensive and not robust enough to attract users. By the same token, an idea must not be too big. Sometimes, fundamental scientific discoveries cannot be reduced to practice within the five to seven year time frame of most venture capital funds.

Regardless of the source of an idea, the critical tasks for the founders of a startup company are to:

- Determine if the idea is big and disruptive.

- Measure the size of the market opportunity.

- Obtain as much patent protection as possible.

- Describe the idea in terms that are understandable and attractive to investors.

- Create a business around the idea that will attract capital.

The NovaDigm ALS3 vaccine is a good example. What makes this vaccine attractive as an investment opportunity? It may be able to prevent both staph (MRSA) and candidiasis infections. Centers for Disease Control data as of April 2016, shows an annual total of 72,444 MRSA infections in the U.S.[1] According to the Centers for Disease Control, candidiasis infects approximately 46,000 people in the U.S. each year, with an estimated attributed mortality of 19-24 percent.[2] Further, the vaccine has the potential to solve the drug resistance problem, because it does not give a pathogen enough time to adapt and resist treatment. For most biopharmaceuticals, the ultimate question is "Does the opportunity have the potential for $1 billion in sales per year?" This is roughly the threshold required by the large pharmaceuticals to justify the enormous investment they must make to acquire a drug and march it through FDA clinical trials to market approval. In the case of NovaDigm ALS3, The answer is a confident yes. The vaccine does appear to have this potential, possibly in more than one market. At this writing, the company has completed one Phase II clinical trial, and it must pass additional clinical trials in order to succeed.

In 1995, the DRC (Reconfigurable Computing Technology) idea of being able to re-architect a computer's hardware at run time, seemed to me to have the potential to dramatically change the way computing was done. Several companies introduced field programmable gate arrays (FPGAs), which were a primitive way of altering a computer's configuration, but it seemed to me that Steve Casselman's reconfigurable computing would help the FPGA companies drive a wedge into the conventional methods for computer chip manufacture. I believed that this was a potentially disruptive technology.

Every company that I become involved with must offer a disruptive technology, or I do not work with it. An example of a promising product with disruptive potential is LiveSafe, a crime reporting app for the smart phone. This app has the potential to shift 911-style telephone crime reporting to a smart phone platform that enhances the conventional phone call with video, photographs, and sound recordings. Will LiveSafe be the company that causes this change? We'll see. Markets are competitive. But, if it is adequately funded, LiveSafe might have a pretty good chance.

Technology Transfer Today

Technologies developed at universities and research institutes can be a good source of ideas for new startup companies, but the "value extraction" processes are not always well understood by the participants.

> **" Don't mistake activity for achievement. "**
>
> —Dan Oswald, The Oswald Letter

It is important that a technology transfer office understand the difference between activity and achievement. In my experience, people who seek to commercialize technologies often get buried under the tasks related to out-licensing patents. They do this by contacting any company that might conceivably have an interest in a specific technology and by endlessly attending corporate partnering conferences in which, presumably, corporations will look at their patent portfolios and license the ones that fit strategically with their business.

The answer is not the activity of licensing, but the creation of value. Let's explore what this means in daily practice.

I have been a part of this process in three different institutions, and my experience would suggest that licensing "raw" patents is not only difficult, but also not terribly profitable. When I have approached corporations about licensing patents, their response has been:

"We won't sign a nondisclosure agreement."

"Have all of the patents been granted? (That's your only protection.)"

"Can you show us a working prototype?"

One project involved a device called a radiation needle, which had been developed for an aerospace application. It appeared to have some application in cancer treatment, because it could deliver an effective dosage of radiation to a very specific location within a tumor. The inventors had a prototype of sorts, but they could not demonstrate that it worked in humans. So all of the medical device manufacturing companies backed away. They wanted to see a working prototype.

Technology patents are like crude oil; their value must be extracted by as process similar to refining. Some of the critical steps involved in creating value based on a patent are:

- Establishing the uniqueness of the idea by performing a full patent file search.
- Determining potential product and service applications for the technology protected by the patent.
- Determining the business potential of the different product and service possibilities.
- Developing a complete and realistic business plan.
- Assembling an initial implementation team.
- Getting to proof of concept.
- Creating a realistic plan for financing the business.

Measuring Value

One of the problems faced by technology transfer offices is that they often do not know how to measure the potential value of the technology they own. How can you create and extract value if you don't know what it is?

Measuring value is fairly simple, once you have a business plan. But the more difficult problem is often deciding what the business plan should be for a specific technology.

> In 2002, I was asked by the CEO of L.A. County Research Education Institute (now Los Angeles Biomedical Research Institute) to assist in negotiating the sale of a royalty-bearing license for a drug called Aldurazyme. This drug is a treatment for "Hurlers Syndrome," a genetic disorder of metabolism which incapacitates the young. The drug was developed at the Research & Education Institute (REI, now LA BioMed) and then licensed to another company. REI wanted to monetize the contract by exchanging its future royalty privileges for cash.
>
> Knowing that the venture capitalists would base their offer on some form of discounted cash flow calculation, I created a net present value model for the expected revenues and profits from the drug. This model helped REI focus the discussion on specific assumptions, such as patient population, pricing of the drug, and market growth, rather than simply requesting an arbitrary dollar amount for the license. The model facilitated the negotiation, and it helped REI get a very attractive price for the license.

Finding and Creating Value

In order to create a working prototype, it is necessary to do many of the things that are required to start a new company: assemble a team of experts, get some funding, plan a development process, and manage that process. So there is almost no difference between extracting value from a patent and building a new startup company around that patent.

For many patents, it is not obvious what products could be built using the technology. Generally, the first step is to identify a list of potential products. The next step is to identify the economic opportunity for each product, which requires a certain amount of sophisticated market and competitive analysis. In my opinion, if an institution is going to patent a technology, it should do what patent attorneys call a "full file search," in order to gain a clear understanding of any prior art. Failure to do this often results in a limited number of claims being awarded and a series of continuation patents, which ends up costing more than the proper process.

Who does the file search and the market analysis? I recommend that these functions be performed within a technology transfer/commercialization organization, but few have the capacity to do this kind of work. Most do not employ people who know how to create the value required to make the technologies attractive to potential licensees.

Extracting Value

The processes of technology transfer and technology commercialization are similar to those we have described for creating successful startup companies. The value of a blockbuster patent or technology increases as different milestones are achieved. To illustrate, the value at different stages in the process might be:

Raw patent or technology: less than $500,000

Proof of concept exists: less than $1 million

Qualified management team and realistic business plan: $2–4 million

Prototype product and beta customers: $3 million or more

Proof of business model: $2–4 million or more

Product ready to introduce to market: $3–5 million

Working product and satisfied customers: $5–10 million or more

Repeat customers, ready for investment to accelerate growth: $10 million and up

$5 million or more in sales and a candidate for acquisition: $50 million

$25 million or more in sales, rapid growth and profitable: $100 million and up, possible IPO candidate in an attractive IPO market

Raw technology has little or no value. For proven blockbuster technologies, the sky is the limit once the value is created.

In my opinion the technology transfer process should be a multistep process: Before incurring the cost of filing for patents, institutions should ask if there is potential economic value. Not that every patent has to have economic value, but if the institution wants to monetize technology, it should ask this question before filing the patent application.

One of the challenges of extracting value from patents is that it can be very difficult to identify the possible products and applications that could be based on a technology. Exploring the potential uses of a technology can require extensive product planning, market analysis, and competitive analysis.

But most technology transfer or technology translation organizations do not have the capability to perform these tasks.

In the case of IC Sensors, which used a university-developed technology to build micro-machined devices, including a micro-sensor, an extensive marketing and analysis effort was required to sort through dozens of applications and settle on accelerometers for automobile airbags. For DRC, it took several years of exploring micro-trading (the idea of arbitraging small movements in stocks on different exchanges), oil exploration, and government security to finally settle on gene sequencing as the attractive application.

Conclusion

The notion of a fundable idea derives directly from the venture capitalists' statistical need for a few homeruns in their portfolio. They need some of their investments to return many multiples of the original investment to make up for the deals where they lose all or most of their capital. Hence the search for big and disruptive products. They know that not every product will live up to these expectations, but if they don't seek technologies, or products, that have the potential, they will not meet their portfolio goals.

In chapter 8: "The Fundable Management Team," we will explore the second critical ingredient of a fundable startup: the fundable management team.

CHAPTER 8

The Fundable Management Team

> "The best CEOs I know are teachers, and
> at the core of what they teach is strategy."
>
> —Michael Porter, "The CEO As Strategist," in *Strategy Bites Back*

What are the qualities of a management team that is likely to get funding from either venture capitalists or angel investors? Most investors have learned that, after the quality of a company's big idea, the most important determinant of success is the caliber of the team. Let's explore what this means.

The Fundable Team

The dream team for a startup would be four or five seasoned C-level executives who are also capable of rolling up their sleeves and doing real work, such as writing computer programs, designing circuits, or designing and testing biochemical compounds, for example. The ideal team would consist of a financial executive, a chief marketing and sales officer, a chief technical officer, and, in some companies, a chief manufacturing officer. But trying to find such a high-level team presents a founder with the most difficult chicken and egg problem. How do you attract a team without money? How do you attract money without a team?

In their early days, most startups require a team of implementers who must develop some proof of concept, if not a working product. A good strategy can be to build the team from the bottom up. This means recruiting some highly talented developers and implementers to begin to create value for the company. Once initial value is created and the company has a better chance of attracting capital, attention can turn to attracting C-level executives.

There is a strong argument, of course, for building the team from the top down instead. The C-level executives might prefer to recruit their own staff. In a perfect world, this makes sense. The challenge is that most startups can't afford to hire a C-level team right away. And the last thing they need is a team of senior executives sitting in offices and collecting salaries when there's work to be done. If a less senior founding team can create some initial value, the company is in a much stronger position to attract both higher level managers and capital.

Most of the successful startups that I have observed have, out of necessity, used the bottom up approach to building their teams. An added benefit of this strategy is that it allows the founder to demonstrate her management skills.

The initial needs of a startup company can include:

- Developing software
- Creating a website
- Creating a prototype or working product
- Getting some initial sales
- Obtaining public relations exposure
- Negotiating strategic partnerships

This approach has significant advantages for a fledgling startup:

- It avoids the problem of the founder writing a business plan and trying to raise capital with no value to demonstrate.

- It avoids the problem of trying to recruit C-level managers when there is no value in the company.

- It allows the company to use stock instead of cash to create some initial value in the form of a product or working prototype.

- It allows a startup to create some momentum.

- It demonstrates the founder's ability to manage.

By creating the team from the bottom up, a startup can end up in a much stronger position to attract senior executives and, eventually, capital. In addition, the bottom up approach creates enormous opportunity for younger participants and people who do not have extensive business experience. The important qualification is having a proven skill and ability to complete tasks within a field such as hardware development, software development, sales, marketing, or public relations. Whether the team is built top down or bottom up, there will be a time to think about recruiting a CEO.

What Does a CEO Do?

There is a simple logic behind the necessity to hire an experienced CEO and managers for a startup. Most capable CEOs devote at least fifteen years and a lot of hard work to their careers before they reach the top level. Here's a sampler of the skills a CEO must possess.

Strategic Planning

If leadership is one of the most important talents of a CEO, then strategic and operational planning follow close behind. Planning is a rich and complex field. Some business development executives spend an entire career developing skills in strategic and operational planning. To me, the distinction is that strategic planning relates more to longer term and competitive positioning goals, while operational planning focuses on short term actions required to achieve long term goals. Planning has its own language for describing goals, objectives, constraints, and action plans. It also has well developed processes and procedures for creating a variety of different kinds of plans.

Corporate Planning

A planning executive might spend years learning the vocabulary and processes of strategic and operational planning. Planning also involves a mindset that is not easily attained. Experienced planners achieve a balance between precise forecasting and establishing realistic and achievable goals. The best plans are ones that are defensible and well supported. Neither overly conservative, nor overly aggressive. The keys are keeping it real and achievable.

Competitive Analysis

Like planning, competitive analysis is a discipline that is learned. The bible for competitive analysis is Harvard professor Michael Porter's original book on the subject, *Competitive Strategy*.[1] This book outlines a detailed process for organizing information related to an industry: vendors within the industry, buyers, suppliers, potential substitute, or alternative, products, companies entering the industry for the first time, and alternative approaches to solving the same problem that the product solves. Porter's point is that competition doesn't only come from other similar products. A substitute for a butane fire-starter, for example, is a match. An alternative product might be a cigarette lighter. An alternative approach to solving the same problem might be using flint and steel to start a fire. It would be shortsighted to plan for a fire-starter business without considering these other options. Porter also outlines approaches for determining the competitive dynamics between existing vendors and describes competitive strategies that a new entrant might pursue in order to establish a position within the industry.

Hiring Personnel

The right team members can make or break a startup. Hiring them requires careful definition and description of each job to be filled. Recruiting must include systematic identification of qualified candidates, careful screening and interviewing of the candidates, thoughtful selection of the most qualified candidates, and reference checking to select among the finalists. Inexperienced managers have a tendency to recruit anecdotally, that is, through their personal contacts. They recruit people they know or the first candidate they meet. This approach may fill the spot quickly, but it rarely finds the best person for the job.

Supervising Personnel

If hiring employees requires *strong* people skills, then supervising them requires *extraordinary* people skills. Motivating, incentivizing, tasking, and overseeing employees calls for skillful communication, expert follow up, and strong management instincts and skills.

Dismissing Personnel

No one wants to bring members into a team and then have to ask them to leave, but a strong manager must determine which team members are pulling their weight and which ones, if any, need to be replaced. An experienced CEO is goal driven.

She has a clear vision of the company's objectives and a good understanding of which team members are contributing and which are not. At times it is necessary to decisively reorganize the team, possibly asking one or more members to leave. Termination is a challenge for any executive, but an experienced executive, who has probably been through it in the past, will have a better understanding of the process.

Team Building

Team building is one of the most important challenges a CEO faces. It involves identifying the key skills required by the first employees of the company, finding people who can have those skills, and then shaping those people into a functioning team. This calls for a combination of executive skills, people skills, the ability to motivate, and knowledge of how best to resolve issues and solve problems. Team building can be extremely challenging for even the most experienced executives.

Complex Problem Solving

A CEO spends a lot of time solving problems. Making the necessary decisions to solve those problems effectively is never easy. It usually involves a process of analyzing the problem, gathering information, processing the information, and deciding on a course of action. The best CEOs achieve an effective balance between gathering information vs. analyzing it and making a decision. The problem, of course, is that there is never enough time to thoroughly analyze the data. An experienced CEO, then, becomes adept at using his judgment while balancing analysis and decisiveness to arrive at a fully supported solution.

A few months after I joined Scientific Data Systems (SDS), it was acquired by Xerox Corp. As events unfolded, I began to realize that I was pretty good at "reading the tea leaves." My instincts for business decisions seemed to be fairly accurate. This wasn't a skill that I consciously fostered. I wasn't doing a lot of in depth analysis of events and possible outcomes. I mostly tried to keep an open mind and imagine how various decisions might play out. I bring this up here, because I believe that one of the keys to being a good leader is having well-developed instincts.

It can be argued that making good business decisions is a matter of gathering the relevant data and processing it appropriately. Executives must often resort to their basic instincts to make important decisions.

Working with a Board of Directors

It is difficult for a person who has never been a CEO or served on a board of directors to understand the dynamics between a CEO and his board. Some boards are handpicked by the CEO so the relationship is relatively conflict free and the board tends to rubber stamp the CEO's decisions. However, this is often not a healthy situation, and it would not be tolerated by most investors.

The boards of most venture-capital backed companies are independent boards in the truest sense; the CEO reports to the board of directors and the board has the right to replace the CEO at any time. The board's focus is on the overall accomplishment of objectives, the financial performance of the company, the strategic directions of the company, and the achievement of long-term goals. The CEO's job is to provide objective information to the board, to work closely with the board at setting goals, and to assume the overall management of the company. Most board decisions are unanimous. I have seen very few issues resolved by a 4:1 or 3:2

vote. This happens because most boards are thoughtful and communicative, and they work hard to find solutions that appeal to all members.

Working with Lawyers

Working with lawyers is not easy for some executives, though I am not sure why. They may have had a bad experience with an attorney, so they tend to shy away from them. More often, the executive thinks she knows the correct and legal answer to a question. But this is dangerous thinking. Lawyers are not cheap, but executives would be well advised to talk to their attorney more frequently. I have worked with dozens of lawyers on dozens of contracts and investment documents and I have learned a lot about their profession. But my greatest lesson learned is to not play lawyer myself. The law is not necessarily intuitive. A CEO should take the lead in making business decisions, but should be quick to consult an attorney if there is any conceivable question about the legality of an action or decision or the best way to address an issue.

Financial Analysis

A CEO does not have to be a financial expert, but he must understand the tools of financial reporting and analysis. This includes interpreting profit and loss statements, balance sheets, and cash flow statements and understanding their implications for the business. The CEO certainly should understand the differences between a company that is solvent and one that is not. Finally, a startup CEO must be familiar with the methods for valuing a company using analytical tools such as discounted cash flow and net present value.

Developing Finance Strategy and Valuing Companies

One of the most important tasks of a startup CEO is to determine the company's cash needs and find ways to satisfy them. Financing strategy for a startup is milestone-driven. It is important to identify the most important value-adding and risk-reducing milestones. Financing objectives should be:

> To provide enough capital to operate the company for twelve to eighteen months.

> To provide enough capital to achieve significant milestones so that it's next round of financing can be completed at a higher valuation, based on value added and reduced risk.

Negotiating

Startup CEOs must be good negotiators. They negotiate employee agreements for members of the team. They negotiate salaries (preferably deferred) and percentages of stock ownership with team members. They negotiate "terms of engagement" with accountants, lawyers, and other vendors. They may negotiate a lease for office space. Ideally, startup CEOs will negotiate an angel or venture capital investment in the company. They need, at a minimum, to be able to obtain fair and reasonable terms in all of these negotiations, and they must have reliable information about market rates for the different services. The bottom line is that the CEO must have strong enough negotiating skills to get the best values for the company.

I helped to sell a TRW division comprised of thirty-five international distributorships. This experience taught me a lot about negotiating. My managers were highly skilled at negotiating, and I learned some important lessons about valuing companies, as well as how to "sell" a proposition. We were able to persuade a buyer to pay $115 million in cash by showing them that it would cost them more to build a similar business internally. Sometimes you have to do the other company's strategic planning homework.

The Role of Chairman

Deciding who should serve as chairman of the board of directors of the company can be complicated. Some CEOs double as the chairman of the board of directors. Other possible choices are the lead investor or a senior industry expert. One approach that a first-time CEO might consider is to involve a very senior and qualified director as a mentor and chairman. I have seen this relationship work well.

The chairman of a startup company often spends a significant amount of time acting as the company's "chief psychologist." Bringing a team of founders together for the first time is not easy. It can involve substantial conflict between team members, and it falls on the chairman to diplomatically resolve issues. The most effective chairmen are usually senior executives who have had experience resolving a wide range of personnel conflicts.

Why CEOs Focus on Proof of Concept

One of the most important questions a CEO must ask about her company's technology or product is, "How do we know it will work?" Venture capitalists and other investors are reluctant to get involved in projects if there is significant risk that the technology or product might not work as expected. They are not interested in funding never ending research projects. Once a concept is proven, however, investors will be more willing to fund product development and costs of introduction to the marketplace. So, a startup company has the challenge of proving that its technology can work. Sometimes government grants can be used to develop a working prototype. If these funds are not available, the startup company may rely on funds from friends and family, or an angel investor who is willing to accept more risk than most.

For some companies, proof of concept might be expanded to include the business model. In this case, the question shifts from will the technology work to can the company be profitable with its business model? In recent history, we have seen some major companies such as Amazon and Google whose business models have been simply to collect as many "eyeballs" (visitors to the website) as possible and find a way to monetize them later. Investors are not always willing to take this risk. They may want some kind of proof that an internet startup can generate advertising revenues or attract new customers at the expected cost.

The Fundable Management Team Understands "Business"

Stan Pace, former CEO of TRW, had an eloquent philosophy about business: "Business is simple; tell me what you're going to do, and do it." Founders and CEOs would do well to heed this advice. It is an important aspect of trust between a manager and her people. It's easier said than done, of course. "Tell me what you're going to do" usually requires an enormous amount of planning and presentation of plans. And "do it" can involve significant execution and management efforts. The fundamental principle of trust between manager and employee—or board of directors and CEO—is invaluable.

Company-Building Skills

As if developing the skills needed by a CEO weren't enough, there is an additional skill set that is required to build a company—

one that many CEOs have not developed. It's possible for a very capable executive to have years of CEO experience but to never develop the following company-building skills:

- Forming a corporation.

- Identifying and recruiting a founding team.

- Deciding how to allocate founder shares to the initial team.

- Creating a first plan for a new business.

- Finding the resources (lawyers and accountants) to incorporate and create effective articles of incorporation and shareholders' agreements.

- Providing leadership in the early stages when a company has no capital.

- Understanding investment deal structures and raising seed capital on terms that won't affect future fundraising.

Company-building skills are specific techniques involved in launching a startup. They are not necessarily skills that an experienced CEO would have unless he has been the CEO of a startup company. Can a CEO with large-company experience possess the resourcefulness and problem-solving skills to work through them? Probably, but a leader who has dealt previously with these issues will almost always do a better job. It's one thing to write a business plan for an ongoing business when you simply update last quarter's, or last year's, business plan. It's very different when you have to create a business plan starting with a blank piece of paper.

These are not skills that a CEO normally acquires in the context of a large company, because the CEO of a Fortune 500 company would probably never have to perform the basic startup tasks.

They are not necessarily intuitive, which is a reason that many first-time founders make mistakes that are often fatal. One common error, for example, is trying to save money by listening to personal advisers instead of getting professional advice from accountants and lawyers. More than one startup has failed for this reason.

The Successful First-Time CEO

There are exceptions to every rule, even to our rule that experienced CEOs make the best leaders. There are some very talented individuals who lack experience as a CEO but are nevertheless able to work through the issues required to build a startup company. These people are rare, but they do exist and they are usually people with extensive management experience. What are the characteristics of these special people? What makes them able to succeed where so many inexperienced CEOs fail?

To define the qualities of an effective first-time CEO we could start with the qualities of an experienced CEO and relax the requirements a bit. The successful "almost CEO" must have most of the following qualities:

- Executive skills, whether learned or natural
- Effective communications skills
- A keen sense of her own weaknesses and a willingness to ask for help in those areas
- Good people skills
- Clear thinking and an ability to focus on important goals
- Ability to prioritize

A universal quality of the successful first-timer is that she knows what she doesn't know. The successful first-timer is generally a mature individual who is very realistic about her limitations and is comfortable asking for help in areas where she needs it. She builds a founding team that complements her own skill set and is strong in areas where she is weak. Doing this requires a high degree of personal confidence, a very healthy ego, and an ability to work comfortably with a multidisciplinary team of experts.

Successful first-timers usually have extensive management experience, although not necessarily at the CEO level. They are experienced at managing people and dealing with the day-to-day dynamics of an organization. They are able to gather information and make decisions in a timely manner. They can articulate the goals of an organization, and they understand how each team member fits into the company's management processes.

Successful first-timers are usually good strategic thinkers. They have a clear vision of their company's potential. They have good analytic skills, meaning that they are able to develop good strategic plans, operating plans, and competitive positioning strategies. Many have developed good selling skills, are able to present persuasively, and are comfortable hiring and terminating employees.

The successful first-timer often works with a mentor or adviser, and he may form a board of directors or advisers that complements his skills. Most are also assertive, but within the constraints of their complementary team. They may be aggressive leaders, but they take advice from their team.

It would be impossible to overstate the importance, for a successful first-timer, of knowing what he doesn't know. This is a rare but often make or break quality in human beings. Most of us think we have a lot of answers and are eager to pursue our own visions of reality, which too often traps us inside the box. But an occasional successful first-timer reaches beyond his inexperience by tapping the wealth of knowledge of a more experienced team.

In the class of first-time CEOs we include a few rare individuals who were able to grow into their job. This would include Steve

Jobs, who returned Apple to profitability after returning as the CEO for the second time in 1997. What kind of skills would an inexperienced CEO need to be successful in her first assignment? Let's look at Lori Torres as a candidate.

CASE STUDY

First-time CEO Lori Torres

Lori Torres is a good example of a CEO who is likely to succeed without having stepped on every rung of the management ladder. Her extensive management experience in a large property management company, combined with her native intelligence and persistence, are helping her build Parcel Pending, Inc., a company with a solution to the problem of delivering packages to large residential living complexes. Currently, shipping companies make a large pile of parcels in the reception area of an apartment compound, creating a security issue and making it difficult for residents to locate their packages. Lori's motto is, "Every problem has a solution. If you have a plan, you can find a solution."

Lori is one of the many successful people who did not have a college education. She says, "I had every reason to not succeed." After high school, Lori got involved in different projects by approaching the people around her who were busy with their own projects and offering to help.

Having spent a number of years assisting others, Lori is now comfortable asking other people to help her. For Lori, the first step in building a business is to write a business plan. "Then you have to network and follow up persistently to find the help you need. I'm very persistent."

Lori worked her way up to senior vice president of property operations of the Irvine Company, an extremely large property management firm in California. She was responsible for 44,000 residential units and 1,200 employees. In that capacity, Lori launched a number of strategic initiatives, including some in the information technology area. The first reaction of her organization was often that there was no way that the initiative would succeed. Lori says, "I didn't let that answer be an answer for me. I don't believe in taking 'no' for an answer."

Having spent a lot of time in residential real estate, Lori was keenly aware of the problem of delivering packages in an orderly and secure manner to large apartment complexes. She invented a computerized system of lockers that would allow delivery personnel to place a package in a locker. The system would then email the resident with the locker number and a secure access code. Lori's system is an elegant solution to a difficult and complex problem.

Lori's persistent networking to find the resources she needed led her to some of the members of Monday Club. With the help of the Monday Club and Tech Coast Angels she was able to raise $1.25 million to help launch her business.

One of her first challenges was to find a low-cost manufacturing firm. She overheard the first name of the owner of a low-cost Chinese manufacturing firm during a casual conversation. With persistent searching on Ali Baba, she was able to find the firm and establish contact, which led to a manufacturing contract.

Lori says, "it's about "problem-solving. I solve problems every day. If you don't know the answer, make it up. You have to start somewhere." Another of Lori's insights is, "It all comes down to finding resources that can help you succeed."

Recently, Lori was trying to solve an inventory management problem, because she is dealing with relatively small numbers of units of different colors. Through some of her networking, she found the name of an inventory management expert who was able to help solve this problem.

Lori says, "In order to succeed, you have to follow up on every referral. There is no problem I can't solve. I just have to find the right people to help."

"It's fundamental human nature that people want to help other people. I'm so grateful for the help I have had. My advice to entrepreneurs is, 'Get feedback from people who know what they're doing and act on it.'"

Lori's next challenge is to make some changes in the Parcel Pending sales force and approach. With persistence and help from her network, I'm pretty sure she will succeed.

(From my September, 5, 2015, interview with Lori Torres,
Founder of Parcel Pending, Inc.)

Entrepreneurship or Management?

The definitions of entrepreneurship, management, and leadership are known, but commonly get intertwined. Let's take a closer look.

Entrepreneurship vs. Company Building

For years, I have asked myself whether good entrepreneurship is enough to build companies. Or is something more required? While I have tremendous respect for entrepreneurs and the teaching of entrepreneurship, I believe that creating successful high-tech companies requires skills that reach beyond the conventional meaning of entrepreneurship.

The term "entrepreneur" connotes a person who has a vision for a new product and extraordinary passion for implementing that vision. This probably helps to explain why a few of the most successful founders, like Bill Gates and Steve Jobs, have outperformed the more conventional VC-backed approach. There is no question that a founder who "owns" a unique vision and is determined to "make it happen" can be a formidable leader.

The dictionary defines an *entrepreneur* as "one who organizes, manages, and assumes the risks of a business or enterprise." Clearly, by this definition, a CEO that meets the requirements of venture capitalists for funding is an entrepreneur. But is an entrepreneur necessarily a leader or a company builder? The emphasis in entrepreneurial training is on the passion, the corralling of resources, and the persistence required to jump one hurdle after another. The emphasis seems to be more on individual performance and not so much on teamwork, company building, and the management of an organization. Not all entrepreneurs have company-building skills.

Does training in entrepreneurship teach the skills required to build a successful company? Not, necessarily, in my opinion. It is certainly possible to teach some of the building blocks, such as finance, accounting, competitive analysis, and market analysis. But the people skills required for success as a CEO usually require years of experience to acquire. Having the skill to make good hiring decisions, to manage C-level executives (COO, CFO, CMO, etc.), to interact effectively with a board of directors, to provide confident leadership under stress, and to be an effective negotiator are not skills that are easily taught, although some extroverts do have natural leadership skills.

In the arena of high-tech business startups, leaders with entrepreneurial talent, but no CEO track record, are often not rewarded with a capital investment.

I have been on the advisory board for the Entrepreneurial program, now named The Lloyd Greif Entrepreneurial Center of the Marshall School of Business at The University of Southern California (USC), since 1984. This connection has been energizing and extremely beneficial for me and my business. I have had at least 15 MBA interns from the program, who have been most helpful in my work with startup companies. I have also lectured to classes, judged business plans, and attended many exciting business plan awards banquets. Through my connection with USC, I taught a class in entrepreneurship. I have developed an appreciation for the teaching of entrepreneurship and the extent to which entrepreneurship and corporate leadership overlap. My son, Brad, and his wife, Karen, manage a very successful "lifestyle" business that Karen started as her senior year business plan project at USC.

An entrepreneur's vision, passion, and determination are essential to the success of a high-tech company, but they are rarely sufficient for building a disruptive business. Most successful high-tech companies combine a strong dose of entrepreneurship with an equally strong dose of executive leadership and company-building experience.

Networking to Assemble Resources

A startup leader must assemble the resources required to build her business. An experienced leader has an advantage, because she is more likely to have an extensive network of contacts. But, whether the leader is experienced or not, she will probably do a lot of networking in order to find resources. There is no shortage in the high-tech startup world of worthwhile networking opportunities.

The best networking opportunities help a leader find people who can help build his business. This includes people who might serve on her board of directors, or industry experts, or people who might become part of her management team. It would not include people seeking to be paid for helping to find resources. Leaders don't need to pay for this kind of help, or pay people who claim they can help find capital.

Two of the best networking models I know are Connect, a San Diego networking group for entrepreneurs and investors, and Monday Club, an 850-member California mentoring network that I founded in 1984, with chapters in Orange County, Los Angeles South Bay (Torrance), and Santa Monica (Silicon Beach).

The original Connect model was simple and effective. It gave entrepreneurs an opportunity to mingle with other entrepreneurs, successful CEOs, business service providers, and investors, to meet people who could help build their businesses. The meetings were simple mixer meetings where individuals had substantial opportunity to get to know each other.

Monday Club meets monthly. At each meeting, two companies present their business plans to the three chapters. They also network extensively with the members. The advertised purpose of these meetings is not to raise capital. Rather, it is to give the presenters useful feedback on their investor presentations in order to improve their *chances* of raising capital. Another objective is to give the presenters an opportunity to meet people who can help with their businesses. Most presenters are in the early stages of the fundraising process.

Monday Club has provided useful feedback to hundreds of companies, many of which have found individuals who can help build their businesses—including both directors and advisers. One company created its entire board of directors by selecting members of Monday Club. Many presenters have also been successful in raising capital.

One reason Monday Club is effective is that the members are hand-picked for their ability to provide useful feedback to the presenters. The members ask good questions and provide feedback almost as informed and valuable as comments the presenter would receive from a venture capital firm. Presenters value the members' feedback because they know that the members are experienced high-tech company builders.

One lesson learned from Monday Club is the extraordinary value of networking for startup companies. It is important for them to meet lots of people in hopes of finding qualified advisers.

Networking events that promise funding or strategic alliances for a startup company are rarely effective. Professional investors often attend these events only to network with each other. Venture capital firms are typically represented by associates, rather than by full partners. Corporations that attend are likely to be assessing competition, rather than planning to make a deal. Financial sources at a "meet-the-money" event are more likely, in my experience, to be investment bankers or finders.

The best way to find the right investors and strategic partners is with a targeted and systematic networking process.

CASE STUDY

Love is Lovelier the Second Time Around

66 The spectacles of experience;
through them you will see clearly a second time. 99

—Henrik Ibsen, *The League of Youth*, Act II

Few companies have a second chance at getting funded. Here's a story about one that did, and it illustrates one of the fundamental principles of this book: Experienced management teams get the money.

The Dream

Steve Casselman dreamed of building the most powerful computer in the world, knowing that the list of most powerful computers is very dynamic, as newer technologies replace older ones and move to the top of the list.

Steve conceived the idea of reconfigurable computing in 1986, one year after Xilinx introduced a field programmable gate array (FPGA), which made it relatively easy to alter a computer chip. A reconfigurable computer is one whose internal design architecture can be modified while the computer operates, making it possible to create a computer optimized for the execution of every part of a computer program. Steve says, "I was inspired, in part, by Amiga's three-chip processor design based on Motorola's 68000 processor and introduced in 1985." This was the first time a processor had used three chips, and it reinforced the value of putting algorithms directly into hardware, an idea that Steve found intriguing. Steve founded the Virtual Computer Corporation (VCC), and in 1987 he received an SBIR (Small Business Innovation Research) grant to develop a reconfigurable computer. His vision involved compiling code into hardware. He realized that Moore's Law (the notion that the capacity of computer chips approximately doubles every year) had limitations and that 3 GHz would be a difficult speed for computer processors to exceed.

The Hope

According to Steve, his original marketing strategy was build it and they will come, not the first time a technology-savvy entrepreneur assumed that the world would be enamored by his invention. In retrospect, Steve says, "It would have been better to build an application to show the value of the technology."

I met Steve in 1995, when I was chairman of the first Los Angeles Technology Venture Forum. Steve was one of the presenting companies, and he asked me to serve on the board of directors of VCC.

Steve obtained a few military contracts to develop encryption applications. He also worked on a project with Xilinx relating to their PCI (PC interface) board, a driver, and some tools using reconfigurable computing. He also received a contract with Marshall Industries for $500,000. Steve considered Xilinx and Marshall, a distributor, to be potential partners, but, for various reasons, those relationships did not materialize. Steve built a staff of about ten people, but he needed funding in order to expand. I advised him that if he wanted to raise venture capital, he needed to bring in an experienced CEO, but he insisted on running the company himself.

Pounding the Pavement

We wrote an attractive business plan presentation to describe Steve's technology and the business opportunities. The technology was very exciting. It had the potential to increase the performance of a supercomputer by a factor of approximately 150, at a cost of less than $10,000. It could be used to create one of the most powerful supercomputers in the world.

We presented the business plan at several financial conferences, and we had several meetings with venture capitalists and angel investors. We also met with several of the companies that manufacture FPGAs, the computer chips that can be easily re-configured, in hopes of entering into a partnership. In spite of exhaustive efforts, the company was unable to raise capital.

When the dot-com bubble burst in 2000, Virtual Computer Corporation lost its contracts, released its employees, cancelled its office lease, and ceased operations.

Bridge to a CEO

Shortly after the bottom fell out of the high-tech markets, I said to Steve, "I think we can build a company, but we will need to recruit an experienced CEO so we can raise venture capital." To his credit, Steve's response was, "Okay. Do what you need to do."

For some months, working through my network of professional contacts, I searched for a qualified CEO. With help from my network and from several executive recruiter friends, we found Larry Laurich, who had been chief operating officer at Tandem Computer, a very successful Silicon Valley computer company. Larry was looking for a new assignment, and he was glad to work for a few months without salary in order to prepare the company for fundraising.

In 2002, with help from Savery Nash, an attorney I have worked with for decades, I proposed that we could build a company by working with Larry and purchasing the assets of the failed Virtual Computer Corporation. We formed the new company, DRC Computer, and as part of the deal, we bought out one small venture capital investor and a handful of creditors.

After DRC was organized and Larry was installed as the CEO, we began to approach angel investors, but the technology was too complicated for all but a few angels to understand. Perhaps some of the Silicon Valley angel groups would have been more disposed to DRC's technology, because many of the members have previous semiconductor industry experience. But, in Southern California, we found very few angels who were able to understand the value in DRC's approach.

Bridge to Capital

We raised about $100,000 from three angel investors, and, a few months later, Topspin Partners, a venture capital firm, invested $6 million. With these funds, we added some key technical staff people, a vice president of engineering, and a vice president of sales and marketing. Under Steve's technical leadership, we were able to develop a working product, although there were a few significant delays caused by the time it took to detect several especially pesky bugs in the system.

Finally, we obtained a working product, and we were able to approach a number of potential marketing partners in fields that included seismic testing for oil deposits, genomic processing, and "micro" stock market trading.

The sailing was not always smooth after DRC received its funding. There were times when Steve felt that Larry wanted to be too involved in technical decisions. For a short time, the company employed a vice president of engineering who sometimes involved several engineers in technical decisions that, it appeared, could have been made by only one or two people. When the time came to get the company's FPGA to boot up in its socket, it failed.

After several weeks, the problem escalated to the board of directors, who had to decide whether to turn the problem over to one person—Steve—or, alternatively, to the entire engineering organization to resolve. As chairman, I was the tiebreaker on this issue. I voted for Steve to resolve the issue on his own, which, in retrospect, was the correct decision. Sometimes, one talented individual can run circles around an organization, no matter how qualified the members might be.

The 2008 economic collapse was similar to that of 2000. It was difficult to sell DRC's products. On June 8, 2009, DRC was acquired by Security First, Inc., whose focus was more on application development. DRC made good progress under Security First because it began developing more applications, which Steve felt it should have done earlier.

Realizing the Dream and Lessons Learned

Eventually, Steve realized his dream of building one of the most powerful computers in the world. In February 2011, Steve's computer was featured in numerous articles stating that it had set a world record for genomic processing by computer.[2]

Looking back at the DRC experience, Steve says, "I wish I'd had a stronger agreement, giving me more responsibility for technical decisions, in order to reduce conflict with Larry. It was good to have Larry as CEO, but there were some conflicts."

Fortunately for Steve, there are indications that the major chip and FPGA manufacturers are finally buying into FPGAs and the reconfigurable computing concept in a way that they have not in the past. Intel recently purchased Altera, a major FPGA manufacturer, for $16.7 billion.[3]

Serial Entrepreneur?

Steve Casselman says, "I want to start another company and do it right this time." Based on his experience with DRC, he would still like to be the CEO, but he would hire a president to handle day-to-day operations. If he did recruit a CEO he would need to find one who "knows what he doesn't know."

(My interview with Steve Casselman took place on April 4, 2015.)

Steve's experience highlights the reason that so many high-tech startups do not get funded: their CEOs do not have enough experience to attract venture capital. DRC had the same technology as VCC, the same products, the same vision, the same marketing strategy, and, with one exception, the same people. That one exception, a CEO with a successful track record, was the key to getting the company funded.

This is a fundamental premise of this book, and we'll develop it further in later chapters.

Venture capitalists don't usually explain why they decide not to invest. Their explanation, or excuse, is always something like "it's a little too early for us," or "that's not an industry we know much about." What they are unlikely to say is "your CEO doesn't have enough experience," but that's often exactly what they are thinking. VCs don't want to upset anyone, and, besides, they might decide to invest later, so they don't burn bridges. But, make no mistake; VCs prefer to invest in companies that have experienced CEOs.

Do Large-Company Executives Make Good Startup CEOs?

Founders of startup companies sometimes turn to former large-company executives to manage their companies. Does it work? Does it make sense? Sometimes.

Large-company executives have usually worked their way up the management ladder, so they have a lot of management experience. And large companies typically have disciplined and professional management cultures, which can be an advantage.

Here are three tests that large-company executives need to pass if they are going to lead startup companies:

> Can the executive work effectively with individual contributors and first-line managers?
>
> Can the executive work without the benefit of an administrative staff and bureaucratic processes to make decisions?
>
> Does the executive have company-building skills?

Senior executives in large companies manage managers. Managing a startup can be more like project management. A startup company CEO must be involved in almost all of the company's activities. A very hands-on style of management is required, which may not be comfortable for all large-company executives.

Large companies generally march to a slower drumbeat than startups. Decisions must be coordinated with many people. Because greater resources are involved in large-company decisions, more is at stake, especially if the company has public shareholders. Managing greater risk usually means taking more time to make sound decisions. A startup CEO might have to make a decision by himself in a matter of hours or days, whereas a large-company CEO might have weeks or months and the help of support staff.

Large-company executives rarely have the company-building skills referred to earlier. They don't usually learn how to form a corporation, decide on the founding shareholdings, write a shareholders' agreement, or raise capital.

Venture capitalists are willing to consider large-company executives to lead their portfolio companies, but there are reasons that they prefer executives who have a history of successfully building venture-capital-backed companies.

When Xerox bought Scientific Data Systems in 1969, Xerox was a large company by any measure. SDS, though no longer a startup, was still small and very entrepreneurial in style. Over a period of several years, Xerox recruited at least four former IBM executives to manage SDS. The strategy often backfired, because the former IBMers had a difficult time adapting to SDS's slimmer structure and faster pace of operation. The experience made me realize that not all "successful" executives can be effective in a startup company.

What Happens When It Doesn't Work?

In 1988 I made an investment on behalf of 3i Ventures in IC Sensors, a company that manufactured micro-machined products out of silicon. One of their most attractive products turned out to be the accelerometer that triggers an automobile air bag. The accelerometer senses whether the car has hit something or perhaps just came to a quick stop?

There were two conditions for my investment:

> That the CEO replace a family member as the head of data processing
>
> That certain cost-reduction steps be taken

About a year later, neither of these things had been done. I called a meeting of the nonexecutive directors and said, "Am I the only one who is unhappy that these things have not happened?" I discovered that all of the other directors shared my concerns, and at that meeting we decided to form a committee to bring in a new CEO.

Through a lengthy search process, we found a CEO who had an ideal mixture of formal management experience and academic training.

This story has two happy endings!

The first is that we found a highly qualified CEO with a very strong engineering background and a PhD in management. He did an excellent job of cleaning up the problems and identifying several promising applications for the company's technology, one of which led to the acquisition of the company at an attractive valuation.

The second happy ending involved the CEO who was replaced by the board of directors. Several years after the change, at an annual shareholders' meeting, he pulled me aside and said, "That was the best thing that ever happened to me. My golf handicap has come down, and my shares in the company are worth at least twice as much as they were before."

Conclusion

No matter how exciting a startup company's business concept might be, investors know that a skilled management team will be required to build a successful company. And the leadership skills of the CEO will be critical to building the right team. The best way for investors to assess a team's likelihood of success is to look at their past accomplishments in closely related endeavors. Investors know that a long list of skills is required for managers to be successful and that these skills are usually obtained by experience.

In chapter 9: "Where Do Experienced CEOs Come From?" we will take a look at how some managers become CEOs.

CHAPTER 9

Where Do Experienced CEOs Come From?

"As a CEO, I am finding that I have to become a learning CEO. I have to go to school all the time because I am learning new skills that I need to run this company and I am realizing that I am not equipped to just coast, I have to constantly renew my skills."

—Indra Nooyi, *Forbes India Magazine*

Who are the experienced CEOs with proven track records in business who are so prized by venture capitalists? Where do they come from? How do they develop the skills required to build a startup company? Every startup company leader should understand the answers to these questions.

At TRW , I had an interim assignment as the general manager of a small division that I returned to profitability by reorganizing it and reducing expenses and then I sold it to another company. I enjoyed this assignment immensely, but I realized that almost all of the other general managers within TRW were older than me. I was in my early 40s at the time while the they were all in their 50s. The message was clear: If I wanted to be a full-time division general manager, I probably had 10 years or more of waiting and training. CEOs, don't happen over-night. The majority of CEOs of S&P 500 companies are in their 50s. According to a 2002 article in *Forbes*, half of CEOs in the United States spent over twenty years working their way to the top. The average age of a CEO in 2001 was 48.8.[1]

How Does a CEO Learn His Skills?

What are the paths to becoming a CEO? Most CEOs start at the bottom and work their way up through an organization, according to a Spencer Stuart study. The study reports that in 2015 the average age of an incoming CEO was fifty-three, while the average age of an outgoing CEO was sixty-two. Further, 84 percent of CEOs were promoted from within the company.[2] I assume that the focus in this study on leading CEOs accounts for the slightly older age compared to the age of 48.8 reported in the *Forbes* study referenced above. Many started in sales, marketing, finance, or operations and then advanced upward in their companies. Most have degrees in business administration, engineering, or liberal arts. In order to function effectively as a CEO, an executive must have a working knowledge of a company's functional organizations: sales, marketing, engineering, manufacturing, finance, business development, and investor relations. Many years of experience are required to obtain expertise across these various disciplines.

Top executives like Jack Welsh of General Electric and Anne Mulcahy of Xerox worked within their organizations for over twenty years before achieving the level of CEO. These are large companies, but there is a message here: The skills required to be an effective CEO are extensive, and it takes years to acquire them.

Where does an executive career start?

Corporate Employee

Let's begin with someone who is simply an employee in a large company. This work experience teaches corporate culture, and how to be a team member, schedule tasks, develop budgets and plans, and communicate upwards and sideways.

Larger companies have well-developed management cultures, and lower-level employees can receive training very productively. They learn the management culture. They learn how to submit expense reports. They learn how to be part of a team and discuss and plan their weekly activities. They learn to participate in departmental planning processes. They learn team problem solving. They learn the importance of accurate forecasting and financial planning, and of operating within budgets and schedules.

First-Level Management

Let's take a look at the skills a manager develops as he works his way up the corporate ladder.

First-level managers incorporate the lessons learned as a corporate employee, and they learn how to manage a team. They may have to recruit new members of their team, and they may need to replace members of the team who are not performing adequately. They develop job descriptions for new employees, interview prospective new employees, and carefully check their references. They learn to plan and to identify and articulate the mission, goals, and objectives for their teams, and to develop plans for achieving them.

Many executives start their climb up the corporate ladder at the bottom rung of sales management, which is extremely important to a company because the sales manager represents the company's lifeline: revenue. If sales managers fail, their companies fail, because they run out of cash. Effective sales managers learn how to assign tasks to their employees and follow up to be sure those tasks are completed. A challenge for sales management is that there can be thousands of reasons why an employee did not perform on plan. Simply put, there can be thousands of reasons that the customer did not buy the product.

Good sales managers ask hard questions. They double-check the answers. They compare answers from one salesperson to another to learn as much as possible about their product's strengths and weaknesses.

Another invaluable skill that sales managers learn is how the customers' suggestions and feedback can help shape new product choices and plans. Salespeople are a company's eyes and ears. They have the closest relationship with customers, and they are in the best position to obtain customer feedback about products, services, and the company's overall performance.

A smaller percentage of CEOs rise up from technical management positions, but they are just as important. An engineering manager, for example, knows the inner workings of the company's products. He is intimately involved in the planning and design of products based on input from customers. He learns the same skills of hiring, firing, motivating, incentivizing, and managing employees as the first-level sales manager.

Higher-Level Management

We use the term higher-level management to refer to managers who manage managers. This is a qualitatively different process than simply managing a team of individual contributors. A higher-level manager who has four direct reports, each of whom manages six individual contributors, is overseeing the activity of 28 people.

At this level, the manager's task is to make sure that the people who report to him directly are managing their people effectively. He must interpret plans and objectives handed down from above by his own superiors, and work with his team of managers to develop plans and strategies for meeting the organization's goals.

As executives who manage other managers work their way up the ladder, there is less change moving from rung to rung. The difference is in the increased responsibility as the employee moves up. In addition, responsibilities become more multidisciplinary the higher the manager moves within the organization.

There may be several levels of sales management, or of engineering, where the focus is entirely on sales or engineering, respectively. But once the executive rises above being a sales or engineering contributor, he needs to understand a broader range of functions. At the highest level of chief operating officer or chief executive officer, the executive needs to have a good understanding of every function within the company, including finance, engineering, sales, marketing, manufacturing, support, and business development.

It would be unusual for an executive to master the skills at any one level or rung in fewer than two or three years. In most companies, there are relatively few opportunities to move up the ladder, and there are usually several candidates competing for the same promotions. Therefore, it is easy to see how it might take an executive 15 years to move up the ladder, even in an organization with only three or four levels of management.

Larger corporations may have ten or more levels of management, which makes it easy to understand why an executive at companies like Xerox, IBM, GE, Merck, or Bristol-Myers Squibb might take fifteen to twenty-five years to work their way to the top rung.

Every rung on the corporate ladder is a place to learn. A company leader who has operated effectively at every level of the process has a significant competitive advantage over one who has never even stepped on the ladder. Venture capitalists understand this. It is the main reason they prefer to invest in seasoned CEOs.

The following case studies show how three distinct executive career paths evolved:

- Dr. Webb Castor followed a sales career path to become a senior vice president of Xerox Corporation.

- Van Honeycutt worked his way from entry level assignments to CEO and Chairman of Computer Sciences Corporation.

- Bryon Merade adopted a policy of "exceeding expectations" to create his own career as CEO of Caldera Medical, Inc.

CASE STUDY

Dr. Webb Castor's Climb to the Top (Almost)

Webb Castor's career path to the top sales and marketing job in a Fortune 200 company is a good example of how unexpected twists and turns occur in the course of a career.

Getting Started

Webb started his career as a Navy pilot and a member of the Navy Cadet Choir, which made appearances on the Ed Sullivan and Arthur Godfrey TV shows in the 1950s.

He had left college at the onset of the Korean War to begin flight training as a Navy fighter pilot. After about five years of active duty, he returned to college to complete his education with a major in English Literature, and a minor in biology. He had become engaged during this time, but cancelled the wedding, and instead of entering graduate school, he began ferrying Navy aircraft in the reserve force while doing standup comedy. During one of his shows in Pittsburgh, he met a sales manager for IBM and was recruited to join the sales force. During his three years at the Service Bureau Corporation, which is IBM's customer application development arm, he learned to identify a company's data processing needs and develop applications to meet them.

The Bottom Rung on the Ladder

Webb moved to Honeywell in 1962. Around that time, many IBM sales personnel migrated to Honeywell. Of the 26 people who were in Webb's IBM sales class, 22 had switched to Honeywell during the1960s. Webb started with Honeywell as a salesman in Cleveland; he became branch sales manager in Hartford, Connecticut in 1964; branch manager in southern Connecticut in 1965; branch manager of a very large office in Omaha, Nebraska in 1967; regional director in Minneapolis in 1969, and director of large systems product marketing and planning in Phoenix, Arizona in 1971.

In 1970, Honeywell merged its business with GE, to form Honeywell Information Systems (HIS), and Webb moved to Phoenix as director of marketing and product planning. During this time, he was also involved in the manufacturing of HIS's products. This organization was responsible for marketing the Multics (multiplexed information and computing service), a mainframe timesharing operating system begun in 1965 and used until 2000. Multics began as a research project and was an important influence on operating system development. (Note: In the early 1970s, I worked on the Scientific Data Systems timesharing system, which was patterned, in some ways, after Multics.) The system became a commercial product sold by Honeywell to education, government, and industry.

From the Ladder to the Pit

In 1973 Webb was asked to make a presentation to some representatives of the Shah of Iran about how Honeywell computers could be used to modernize his country. Afterward, he was invited to move to Iran to serve as a senior advisor of a company with that purpose. For a time, he was on loan from Honeywell to ISIRAN (Information Systems In Iran), which later hired Ross Perot to do extensive systems development. ISIRAN installed multiple Honeywell 6000 systems.

While in Iran, Webb worked with a "cousin" of the Shah who was constantly asking for favors. He wanted to make education available to remote areas of the country via satellite, so he asked Webb to make arrangements with Hughes Aircraft for the necessary satellite services. Later Ross Perot's organization became involved in implementing the system, but the system was never completed because it was not possible to deliver nuclear power to the remote areas of Iran. According to Webb, management responsibility in the Iranian system is simple: "If things go well, *they* take credit; if not, *you* take the blame."

Webb says, "The Chief of Naval Operations, Admiral Ahtai, asked me how to put together a 'protected facility.' When I asked for specifics, he questioned my qualifications. I defensively agreed to find him an answer. Knowing the Iranians' propensity to do the biggest and best in the shadow of their paranoia, I gathered resources like Parsons Engineering from the United States and developed a plan for a protected facility which was several thousand feet under a mountain, individually compartmentalized, shock absorbed to 2000 psi, and able to withstand a direct hit from a 100-megaton atomic weapon with 97 percent chance of survivability. When I presented this to Admiral Ahtai, he scanned it briefly, looked up and asked, 'How big a bomb did you say?' I repeated, 'A 100 megaton atomic bomb with 97 percent chance of survivability.' He swept the plans off the table and said, 'Bull ####.' I am not going to war with anybody who has a bomb that big! I just don't want people throwing hand grenades through the window."'In that case,' I humbly responded, 'We don't need to go quite that deep.'"

Webb says, "I guess our proposal was a little overkill."

In 1975 Webb returned to Boston as vice president of national operations for Honeywell. His organization operated like an internal venture capital company; it evaluated new business opportunities, developed selected ones, and managed them.

The Lazy Man

Webb talks about "the lazy man's way to success." He says, "I lifted it from the title of a book written in the 1960s, called *The Lazy Man's Way to Riches,* by Joe Karbo. It was primarily about the technique of visualizing your success. My use of the term is somewhat different, having to do with finding the easiest and most expeditious way to win. Laziness can be a virtue if properly used. For example, in persuading the country of Iran to use only Honeywell computers, rather than facing off with the other manufacturers, I took the high ground. I wrote a letter to the Shah explaining that the purpose of computers in his country had nothing to do with price and detailed capabilities, but rather the combined ability to maintain his forces, in the event of attack, with control and command systems sufficient to regain the offensive. In short, common hardware, software, and trained personal will increase your percent chance of survivability. Cost is not the issue; survivability is the issue. And, since we already had one large computer in his air force, it became a cause to build upon."

Yet Another Pit

Webb received extensive international experience when he found himself dealing with a Mexican company which was part of the Honeywell Bull French corporation. He helped organize the "spinout" of the Mexican company from the

French company into a U.S. firm. This was a very complicated international transaction Involving three nations' different laws and various vagaries of business culture.

During this transaction, Webb had to deal with several issues of international currency. At the time, the Mexican peso was substantially devalued, but Webb was able to hedge against this by converting certain loans to pesos.

One of the products Webb sold during this time was the page printer, a computer printer using heat-sensitive paper. His major competitor for this product was Xerox Corporation. "We outsold them," he says, "only because they encountered too many technical problems at that time."

In 1975, Xerox announced that they wished to sell off the XDS computer division. They had purchased it from SDS in 1969 for almost one billion dollars, and had been unable to develop the company.

Honeywell entered into a contract with Xerox to take ownership of the business, but with no cash payouts other than splitting revenue 60/40, Xerox maintaining the inventory and assets on their books and Honeywell providing sales and field service.

Webb set up a customer board of directors to decide how to spend a portion of the profits of the joint-venture company, to assist their needs. This was very similar to a venture capital deal. Webb's idea of "success the lazy man's way" suggested letting the customers run the business in order to get critical feedback directly from the market participants. "Let the customerhelp you runthe business and he will be successful. And so will you."

At this time, Webb was the head of all the sales and marketing for the combined General Electric/Honeywell businesses. The interaction with General Electric had resulted in a clash of cultures, Honeywell being very aggressive and entrepreneurial, and, GE more staid and by the book.

The Struggle to Move Up

In 1980 Webb left Honeywell and became involved in four different entrepreneurial companies. He says, "We dumped one of the companies and took three public." One, Aviation Simulation Technology, developed and produced the first general aviation digital computer-run simulators. Webb says, "By now, I am sure, it has long been displaced by the desktop or laptop computer." However, the oceanographic company and the architecture and design businesses have thrived.

The Top Rung (Almost)

In 1982 Webb met a headhunter who was trying to fill the most senior sales and marketing position at Xerox. Webb agreed to be interviewed by Xerox, and he accepted the job, becoming became senior vice president of Xerox, reporting to Bob Adams, president of Xerox Systems, responsible for all worldwide sales and manufacturing of systems products.

According to Webb, "David Kearns was the CEO and chairman of Xerox then. My deal with David was that, if I stayed for five years, I would receive a retirement package. In 1984, Xerox merged sales and marketing for the system business, which included desktop devices and printers, with the copier business, and I became sales manager for the western half of the United States for both system businesses and copiers. Shortly thereafter, after my five years, I suggested that my time was up. I was asked to stay on for two more years and wrote a strategic positioning document for Xerox's document strategy. And then I took my retirement package."

*(From my interview with Dr. Webb Castor,
Former Senior Vice President, Xerox Corporation, November 14, 2015.)*

CASE STUDY

Van Honeycutt, former CEO and
Chairman of Computer Sciences Corporation (CSC)

Starting Small

Van Honeycutt's early career interest was the computer industry, primarily in software and technology. His first jobs, in the mid-1960s, were with small companies that provided computerized accounting services such as payroll, general ledger, accounts receivable, and accounts payable. At that time, amazingly enough, companies would receive punched cards from their customers and then process the information on their computers and return the results to the customer.

Van's first assignments were to provide technical support for a sales team. He would analyze the customer's problems and then propose a software solution. The whole idea was to provide better, faster, cheaper and more accurate results by using software. Through these assignments, Van gained an understanding of computer programming, and he learned six different programming languages, including RPG, PL-1, COBOL, and Fortran. His mission at this time was to provide the technical expertise that most of the sales personnel did not have.

In order to get more directly involved in the selling process, he joined Randolph Corporation, a computer services company, which was shortly thereafter acquired by Travelers Insurance. Van realized that he really enjoyed software technology, sales, and marketing. He asked himself, "Where can I work and not have to change jobs every six months?"

Seeking and Finding Opportunity

Van researched companies he thought he might enjoy working for, including Computer Sciences Corporation,

ADP, SBC, McDonald Automation, and Computer Task Group (CTG). In 1971 he joined the Infonet Division (computer timesharing services) of CSC.

Initially, he helped sell Infonet's time-sharing services to government agencies in Washington DC, where he made his home temporarily. He traveled to 12 GSA (General Services Agency) regions to explain Infonet's time-sharing services for engineering and structural engineering. In 1973, Van became branch manager for Infonet's commercial business. He was bidding commercially available services to the federal government and securing many large contracts. After two years, the revenue from the federal business exceeded revenue from CSC's sales to commercial entities, even though Infonet was getting competition from desktop computers running spreadsheet software like Excel and VisiCalc.

By 1975, CSC's government revenue had grown to 75 percent of the company's total annual revenue. The company decided it needed growth in its nonfederal and international business. To achieve this, it expanded its sales effort in Europe. It was especially successful in getting contracts with the European Aviation Safety Agency (Europe's equivalent to the Federal Aviation Administration in the United States).

In 1976 and 1977, Van attended a CSC-wide planning meeting where the company decided to expand both its global and commercial businesses. In order to accomplish this, the company concluded, it needed a better model for acquiring companies. After the planning meeting, CSC initiated a series of very innovative and strategic acquisitions, in which Van was very involved.

The Acquisition Expert

The first company CSC acquired was ITEL, a White Plains, New York computer services company that had purchased numerous other small firms. Van's first top-level management assignment was to manage the post-acquisition ITEL.

CSC's second acquisition was a distribution software company that provided services for Suzuki Motorcycles in California as well as other customers. The third acquisition was another company in New York. Van's assignment was to divest 50 percent of this company's activity because it was inconsistent with CSC's business strategy.

Van's experience in buying and selling companies taught him valuable lessons about how to value businesses and negotiate acquisitions and sales of companies.

Another acquisition was a consumer credit reporting company in Houston. Van moved his family to Houston so he could manage this company. Under Van's leadership, the company advanced from the fourth largest company in its industry to the second largest in six years.

One of Van's reflections on his career is, "You really have to love this stuff. You have to really like what you are doing in order to create a persuasive track record."

CSC made a deal with Equifax in 2005, in which CSC kept its proprietary credit file. This file, which had been created and maintained by CSC, collects public record data for the middle states of the United States. It is a rapidly growing database. Every time Equifax sold a record to one of its customers, CSC received a fee. In 2014, CSC exercised its "put" contract to sell the database to Equifax for an attractive profit.

The Penultimate Rung

Van moved to Los Angeles to run the Business Services Group for about three years. He was promoted to President of CSC, and he joined the board of directors. He became CEO in 1995, and he remained in that position until 2007. From 1999 to 2007, Van was chairman of CSC.

Van believes that the most important lessons he learned were about valuing, buying, and selling companies. He believes that in order to do a good job of these tasks, he needed to understand the technology underlying each business.

Van has been on other boards of directors where he has helped manage CEO succession. He believes that CEOs should be promoted from within and that the best candidates are doers with enthusiasm who know the company's customers well and understand the company's financial statements. He looks for candidates who are deal- and sales-oriented, and who know intimately the company's customers and understand their needs.

Van thinks it's more difficult to sell a service than a product and that this skill became one of his important competitive advantages. He also thinks that he has obtained valuable skills for valuing companies and making strategic acquisitions. He says, "Solving tough problems is an important part of a CEO's responsibility."

In Van's words, "The CEO has to know more about the company than any other employee."

Van developed a reputation for increasing CSC's revenue. When he first joined CSC, the company's revenue was about $2.5 billion. When he became CEO in 1995, revenue had grown to $7–8 billion. When he retired as chairman, CSC's annual revenues were nearly $15 billion.

Overall Van acquired scores of companies for CSC. Van asks, "How could you ever get this experience without going through all this?" Exactly. True leaders have extensive experience, and Van is a superb example!

(From my interview with Van Honeycutt, former Chairman and CEO of Computer Sciences Corporation on November 25, 2015.)

CASE STUDY

Bryon Merade: Following a Success Model and Getting Good Advice

Bryon Merade has spent an entire career creating his own success. Yet, after getting his own company off to a good start, he decided to recruit his own boss—a diversified board of directors to whom he would "report." Here, in Bryon's words, is his story:

> I've been an entrepreneur all my life. It seems to come naturally. When I was eleven years old, I had a paper route. For some reason, I decided to do more than just deliver papers. I decided to exceed expectations. So I asked my customers, "Where would you like the paper delivered?" I found that by asking the customer what they wanted and then doing it, I received much larger tips. Somehow, for me, this was as natural as breathing. I really didn't have to think about it.
>
> When I was in high school, some charitable organizations sold candy to make money. I decided to sell candy to make money for myself. So, I bought candies for $.30 and sold them for $1, making a $.70 profit. I often made $50 profit in a single day.
>
> I spent some time as a cyclist competing against Lance Armstrong. I was in the top 5 percent, but I realized I had to be in the very elite top 1 percent to make any money. So, I went to work for a bicycle warehouse and, after a short time, I asked if I could have a sales job. I asked what was expected of sales personnel, and I worked hard at exceeding those expectations. In this case that meant working much longer hours than the other employees. I had a work ethic that simply allowed me to outperform the others.

At age seventeen, I asked to be promoted to the position of regional sales manager of the bicycle warehouse. The answer was, "No, you would certainly fail." I persuaded the management to create a new sales region where there had not been one before. I was creating my own opportunity. I figured there was no downside and there was a good chance that my work ethic would succeed. Twelve months later, my new region was the largest sales region in the company.

At that point, I decided to try my sales expertise in a new industry—either information technology or healthcare. I went to work for a small company, BEI Medical, manufacturer of gynecological medical devices. In my first month, I was the salesman of the month. Why not? Isn't that what you're supposed to do?

At age twenty, I became a junior sales manager. Then I advanced to middle management and then to director of sales. When I asked for this latest promotion, the CEO said, "I have to cover myself; I can't just promote you, a twenty-year-old, to head our sales team." So he sent me to spend a day with Charlie Crocker, who was chairman of the board. Charlie Crocker said nothing but listened to my story and then he said, "Okay, let's go talk to Dick [the CEO]." Charlie Crocker told him, "Bryon has my full support." So I basically created the opportunity to lead United States sales and customer support.

Again, my strategy was to exceed expectations. I've always agreed with Seneca [the Roman philosopher], who reportedly said, "Luck is what happens when preparation meets opportunity." I saw an opportunity and prepared my case. A good career model is to be deliberate and focused and always exceed management expectations.

After being the head of sales for BEI, I decided to leave and start my own company. I said to the BEI CEO, "I'm leaving and you're going to fund my startup company." After listening to me for half an hour, he did just that.

My idea was to start a medical device distribution business for companies with surgical solutions. All I needed to get started was a place to hang a shingle and a few dollars. Five years later, the company, Caldera Medical, expanded beyond distribution and started developing new products.

I think I have an above-average risk/reward comfort level. I'm not a huge gambler, and I'm not necessarily trying to hit home runs. Also, I'm not in it for the money. I have no desire to be extremely wealthy. When I tell people that, they say I'm full of it. But I'm serious about that. I have a passion for being a leader who helps develop people and businesses. I try to have a positive life-changing impact on someone every day.

My goal at Caldera Medical was to provide a high quality of life for women who have serious surgical needs. Caldera Medical feels like an extension of my paper route. I'm asking customers—in this case, doctors—what they need and meeting or exceeding their expectations.

Initially, Caldera had no product. I started with an advisory board of two urologists, two gynecologists, and a general surgeon. Our area of specialization was urogynecology. We were sure if we could deliver good products, the doctors would listen to our story. We spoke to a lot of urogynecologists and urologists. Our question was, "What one thing would help you and your patients the most?"

We registered to attend the most prestigious medical conference in the country, and then we sent a FedEx package to each of the top ten faculty members at the conference. The package contained a letter inviting the faculty member to meet with us for ten minutes. It also contained an empty box for an expensive Montblanc fountain pen, the implication being, "Meet with us and we will give you the pen."

Nine of the ten faculty members accepted our offer. All nine gave of us much more than the ten minutes we requested. Five of the faculty members became early adopters of the product we decided to develop. Their help led us to approximately $2 million worth of early revenue for our company.

"We said to these people, 'We really want to know what you think. What products do you need? What improvements would you like in existing products?'

One of the principles of operating this way is that you have to embrace failure. You have to be willing to fail. You have to try lots of different ideas with the knowledge that not all of them will work.

Sometimes you have to put yourself in the mind of the other guy. You have to figure out how he is thinking. What are his best outcomes, and how can you help him achieve them? Sometimes I pretend I'm on the other guy's board of directors, and I try to give him the best advice I can think of.

A patent infringement lawsuit filed by a competitor is an example. It was not in the competitor's best interest to push Caldera out of business. They saw some value in a verdict and a royalty award. But I convinced the CEO of the plaintiff company that it would be even better for them to create new intellectual property and get royalty payments on that. I said to the CEO, "This is what your board should be thinking. Discuss it with to your board." Six weeks later the response was, "Yes, we will license the technology to you."

Then I said to the CEO, "Caldera Medical is your best licensee. We are a willing participant and we will deliver benefits." Then I added, "But the license must be fully assignable." In response, of course, the CEO said, "No way. We don't want to create an opportunity for a big competitor to acquire you and then compete with us."

My counter was, "We will only do the deal if the license is fully assignable. You'll only be adding one additional competitor. Again, you should talk to your board of directors." Fortunately, they agreed to this demand and we signed the deal.

When it comes to day-to-day management, that's probably my downfall. I don't really have a "back-up" executive in the company. I should be spending 100 percent of my time on strategy, and I can't.

Why did I decide to create my own board of directors? Most companies have outside investors who then become directors. I wanted to have a proactive board and I wanted to be held accountable for my decisions and actions. And I really wanted the added oversight and leadership. The reason to have a board of directors is to obtain informed, expert, unfiltered, feedback and advice.

I started the interviewing process in 2009, and I began to form the board in 2010. I think I've assembled a good group; all of the people want to be there, and they want to give me good advice. For the first two years we pursued a growth initiative which worked pretty well, but then we ran into a class-action lawsuit similar to those filed against almost all of our competitors.

The company has spent the last several years working its way out of a tangle of class-action lawsuits that have affected the entire industry with respect to certain mesh-based surgical products. Hopefully, we'll be able to get back to our growth strategy pretty soon.

(My interview with Byron Merade, Founder, CEO and Chairman of the board of Caldera Medical, Inc., occurred on November 15, 2015.)

Bryon created his own path to becoming CEO of Caldera Medical; assembling an experienced board of directors has certainly made him a better CEO. It has allowed him to leverage his lifelong strategy of always exceeding expectations. He is a good example of a self-made CEO.

How Do Career Paths Evolve?

When startup company founders decide to be the CEO of their company, they often violate what seems to be a natural law of good careers: they evolve in gradual steps. In my opinion, most great careers progress gradually as a person gains knowledge and experience doing things they enjoy and for which they have some expertise. When founders move from the "laboratory" to a CEO position, they are violating a fundamental principle of good career progression. They are making a chasmic leap, a discontinuity in their career path that, at best, involves significant risk.

I subscribe to what I call the Haney-Karma career path theory: If you're doing something you enjoy and do well, and if you're learning valuable skills, be patient. Your career will evolve in exciting ways. Your accomplishments and your knowledge stick to you and become the essence of your career path.

Starting after my junior year in college and continuing through my graduate school years, I had four summer jobs with IBM as a systems engineer. These jobs gave me enormous respect for the management culture that exists within IBM. Large corporations need a disciplined management culture in order to survive and make things happen. One of my IBM assignments, in New York City, was to write a compiler program to translate IBM 1401 programs into IBM 360 programs. I was impressed that such a large organization used a summertime employee to solve an important problem.

When I graduated from college, I would have laughed at the suggestion that I would one day be a venture capitalist or a founder of companies. But the evolution was natural. From software management, to product planning, to strategic planning, to operational management, and finally to venture capital, angel investing, and company building.

Van Honeycutt suggests that young people should ask themselves the following career-related questions:

- What are your passions?
- What do you really like to do?
- What do you want to be doing in 20 years?
- Where do you see yourself?
- What kind of job?
- What level of management?
- What level of wealth?

Finally, Van suggests that young people get involved with a company that does the things they truly enjoy doing.

Is Serial Entrepreneurship a Path to Being a Successful CEO?

My friend Bob Gottdener, who has worked with a lot of startup companies, asks an interesting question: Can the experience of a serial entrepreneur, even if some of the experience is negative, be a training ground for a good CEO?

It's fairly common at our Monday Club meetings for a presenter to introduce himself by saying something like, "I have had five successful startups." My reaction, sometimes silent and sometimes out loud, is always, then why do you need my money? If your startups were successful, you should have made enough money to provide the seed capital for the next one.

One answer to Bob's question is that sometimes we learn as much from failure as we do from success. Not every learning experience has a positive outcome. It can be difficult, however, to determine if a negative outcome was the fault of the CEO or circumstances beyond her control.

But there is no guarantee that a serial entrepreneur will have developed the extensive skill set required to build a successful business. On-the-job training is not always as sound a master as years of experience in a larger corporation with a strong management culture and a well-defined scorecard.

Conclusion

Most successful CEOs learn their skills over a fifteen to twenty-year period of time. Many start at the lowest level of their company and gradually work their way up the corporate ladder to the CEO position. Others may be able to leverage many years of management experience to make the leap to a leadership (CEO) position. Most successful careers reflect a gradual progression from one level of management to the next and not a great leap across multiple levels of management.

Given the many skills required to be a CEO and a company builder, one can ask whether there is a shortcut to developing these skills. This is the subject of chapter 10: "Is There a CEO Fast-Track?"

CHAPTER 10

Is There a CEO Fast Track?

"There are no shortcuts to any place worth going."

—Beverly Sills, quoted in
Conquering an Enemy Called Average

Tempting Founders

Many founders would like to think they are the exception, but, as we know, there is no free lunch.

A large industry of incubators, accelerators, mentors, job coaches, advisers, finders, and CEO coaches offer first-time founders the promise of a quick path to success. To an inexperienced founder who is passionate about building her dream, these approaches can be extremely seductive. Let's take a look at these strategies and see how likely they are to improve the startup process.

The Incubator Experience

The incubation process offers inexperienced founders a quick path to success. Office space. internet access. Introductions. Other entrepreneurs. Advisers. Business plan assistance. And, presumably, access to capital.

Unfortunately, if a CEO is unfundable at the beginning of a such a process, she is likely to be unfundable at the end as well. It's probably not possible to compress fifteen to twenty-five years of learning into a few months or even years. If there are exceptions, they most likely involve first-time founders who have extensive experience and most of the required qualifications, so that, with a little nudging and coaching, they can be converted into fundable CEOs. In my experience this is extremely rare.

In 1997 I was working with a company that had a promising technology for creating 3D maps of geographic terrain. The founders had good technical backgrounds, but they had no business, strategic, or managerial skills, and they were unable to raise capital. Over the course of several years I helped the company develop a business plan, and I identified a prospective CEO, who was very interested in joining the company.

The CEO candidate had a strong technical background, but he had also been the CEO of several companies. He also felt that he could bring in a few investors if he was appointed CEO.

But at the very last minute, the company severed its relationship with me and the potential CEO and gave up a significant percentage of its equity to enter into an agreement with a large university-sponsored incubator. The incubator promised office space and equipment, conference rooms, internet access, and assistance from lawyers, accountants, and investors. And, of course, the founders liked the idea that they could continue to manage the company.

Predictably, in about six months, the company failed because it was unable to raise capital.

The reason? Simple. The unfundable managers who entered the incubator were the same unfundable managers who appeared in the business plan as "management." No amount of incubation could turn them into fundable managers. The only thing an incubator could have done to help this company was to help it recruit a credible CEO, which, of course, is exactly what I had done.

Sadly, this seems to be the story for most companies that enter incubators. There are probably a few successes, but it seems to me that the best strategy is for the incubator principals to manage the companies and provide a "bridge to a CEO." I find the "bridge to a CEO" concept very useful. If a company can't hire the right CEO at the outset, it can look for ways to build a bridge to a CEO who will attract capital. Building a bridge could mean, for example, hiring a part-time or interim CEO until the company can afford to pay a full-time one.

CASE STUDY

Jeremy Wall on Incubators and Accelerators

Jeremy Wall is the founder of Lumenus, Inc., a manufacturer of safety clothing with embedded internet-connected lighting and warning devices.

In his search for help with his startup he explored many incubator and accelerator approaches, including the leaders in the field such as Y-Combinator and Tech Stars.

Y-Combinator puts small amounts of money into a large number of companies and provides some assistance.

Tech Stars offers $100,000 in exchange for a convertible note to each of its companies upon acceptance. It also invests $20,000 in exchange for 6 percent of each company's common stock. Tech Stars, Jeremy feels, is providing a more extended service with their own internal version of "LinkedIn." It gives its clients access to an elite collection of mentors and camaraderie amongst other TechStars founders and peers.

Jeremy's most recent experience was with ReadWrite Labs an incubator that was working with eleven companies. ReadWrite has a focus on the "Internet of Things," the idea of embedding computing devices in everyday objects so that they can send and receive data. This is exactly Jeremy's territory.

ReadWrite takes 1 percent of equity from each client company. In exchange, ReadWrite Labs gave Jeremy useful assistance, business planning, and connections to their community members in the Los Angeles San Fernando Valley as well as abroad.

Seperately, Lumenus was involved with the Grid110 incubator which offered a very low-touch program and free office space for twelve months in the prestigious Deloitte Tower in downtown Los Angeles.

Jeremy thinks that his three months with ReadWrite Labs was essentially a due diligence period. He feels that most of the incubator's companies will not be able to raise capital immediately after graduating.

Jeremy feels that he got some constructive help from ReadWrite in preparing an investor ready business plan presentation. ReadWrite also used its web site to help promote his presentation to a large conference. He felt that ReadWrite introduced him to some valuable mentors, including some important contacts in China, through their extensive network of connections.

Incubators usually create an expectation that they can help their clients raise capital, but Jeremy did not see many clients get substantial funding. Jeremy saw seventeen peer companies present at two "demo days," but none raised capital.

According to Jeremy, some angels now ask the question, "Have you been through an incubator?" They seem to see graduation from an incubator as a form of validation.

Jeremy also met a few "micro-VC" firms. These are venture capital funds with small amounts of capital, such as ten million dollars. They provide assistance similar to incubators and accelerators, but they can provide larger amounts of seed capital.

Jeremy also explored crowdfunding as a source of capital. He observed a number of companies successfully raise capital from crowdfunding. In some cases, crowdfunding allows a company to create an initial customer base which can be extremely valuable. "If a company can raise $250,000 through crowdfunding it gives the founders confidence to move to the next step."

Jeremy says, "The spray-and-pray approach that many incubators take does not really align well with the founders' objectives. It allows the incubators to sit back and watch the action, whereas the founders must find a way to make their company successful."

Jeremy presented to all three Monday club venues in May, 2017. He felt that he received valuable feedback on his business plan presentation and he met some people that he thinks might be able to help his company.

(From my June 1, 2017, interview with Jeremy Wall, founder of Lummenous, Inc.)

To amplify Jeremy's point about the misalignment of objectives between a startup and an incubator, it helps to think about who has what eggs in what basket. If an incubator puts a little money into a lot of startups, it has an egg or two in each of many baskets. It doesn't matter to the incubator which eggs are successful as long as a few are eventually. But a founder has all of her eggs in one basket, and she is fighting an all or nothing battle to succeed. Her objectives are very different from those of the incubator.

When venture capitalists invest in a company it is true that they probably have eggs in dozens of baskets. But venture capitalists are able to either provide or attract *all* of the resources the company will need to be successful, assuming the company meets its objectives. This is a critical difference.

At this writing, Jeremy is re-focused on creating more value in his company in hopes of eventually attracting the capital he needs. One of his first steps will be to expand his technical team with the addition of a part time software architect who can help expand the product line and its interface to the Internet of Things.

The incubation concept is very seductive. It sounds like a good idea. Incubators have managed to raise large sums of local, state, and federal money to pursue their goals, but I believe the results are pretty predictable and unfortunate. Successes are rare. As Beverly Sills said, "There are no shortcuts to any place worth going."

It's surprising to me that so many incubators and accelerators get public funding when so few have produced measurable positive results. Public officials obviously mean well, but they fall into the same trap as many founders; they don't know to whom they should listen, so they end up listening to the wrong people. The few startups that have truly fundable ideas don't need incubators or accelerators; most would be better advised to get help in finding the right CEO.

Through the eyes of Monday Club, I have observed the behavior of hundreds of advisers, mentors, finders (people seeking to be paid for helping companies find capital), incubators, accelerators, and job coaches. The most successful leaders have the resourcefulness to approach investors directly without the help of middlemen and agents. The recurring theme is, "If a founder doesn't have the executive skills to build a successful company, no process is likely to compress 15-20 years of management experience into a few meetings, or even a few years."

Accelerators

An accelerator is an organization designed to help speed up the growth—or access to capital—of startup companies. It typically does not offer as many services as an incubator, such as office space. An accelerator may help to improve a company's business plan, or try to make useful introductions. It might also try to improve a company's business and marketing strategies. The idea, of course, is to "accelerate" a company's growth.

Any assistance can be helpful, but business plans, marketing strategies, and introductions are rarely the critical impediments to growth or success for a startup company. If a startup has strong and qualified management, it will not need help in developing plans and strategies. If it doesn't, no amount of "accelerating" is likely to make the company attractive to investors. The key question investors will have is still what is the track record of the management team?

An accelerator sometimes helps a company write its business plans or design its presentations to investors. I do not recommend this. A business plan and investor presentations are key communications for a startup. Creating them is an iterative process that requires serious thinking and commitment on the part of the internal team. It is important that the management team *own* the plans, which only happens if they develop them. And investors can usually tell when a business plan has been written by a third party, and they will generally subtract points from the management team.

Mentors, Job Coaches, and CEO Coaches

A mentor, job coach, or CEO coach with extensive company-building experience can be a valuable resource to a startup company. But venture capitalists do not invest in these people; they invest in highly qualified CEOs and managers. The skills needed for success must be vested directly in the startup team, not in a team of surrogates or outsiders.

Can mentors, job coaches, and CEO coaches convert an inexperienced and unqualified CEO into a fundable CEO? If it takes fifteen years of executive experience to before a CEO is "seasoned," it is unlikely that a few months' advice will have meaningful impact on a founder's skills. Investors interface directly with the CEOs of their portfolio companies, which makes it impossible for an inexperienced CEO to carry an adviser around in his hip pocket. It is unlikely that any amount of mentoring or coaching will turn an inexperienced founder into an experienced one.

Are there situations where an experienced and qualified CEO would want the professional assistance of a coach or mentor? Yes. An extremely strong and fundable CEO may want a mentor in order to perform even better. For example, Jim Diller, a veteran former National Semiconductor executive, respected Don Valentine, a top venture capitalist, as a mentor in guiding Sierra Semiconductor to an IPO.

A mentor may also have positive impact, as in the case of "almost CEO," Lori Torres, who we met in chapter 8. A CEO who has 95 percent of the required skills may benefit substantially by having an experienced mentor in his arsenal. Can this help the CEO become fundable? Possibly, but the CEO will have to form his own relationship with investors; his coaches and mentors cannot do it for him.

Finders

A startup company founder is likely to encounter one or more "money finders," who hold out the promise of finding capital for the startup in exchange for a retainer fee and/or a commission. Fortunately, this activity is highly regulated by the SEC and Financial Industry Regulatory Authority (FINRA). According to Richard A. Riley of Hawley Troxell, a Boise, ID law firm, a finder must be a registered member of FINRA, although some finders claim they do not need to register because they qualify for the finder's exemption. But this exemption is very narrow and does not apply to individuals who are in the business of raising capital for startups.[1]

Raising capital with the help of an unregistered finder carries serious risks, not just to the finder, but also to the company's officers and directors, so it should be avoided at all costs.

Can a FINRA-licensed agent improve a startup company's chances of raising capital? In rare cases such an agent might provide a fast track for an inexperienced CEO to get funding, but it rarely works. Most licensed broker/dealers are focused on larger deals and larger commissions.

Venture capitalists generally do not accept deals from finders, because they are aware of the legal issues and because they don't have to. They see enough good investment opportunities that they don't have to pay fees. Besides, they don't want any of their funds to be used to pay commissions; they want all of their capital to go directly toward building value in the company.

Crowdfunding

We looked at crowdfunding in chapter 5. Its increasing influence may provide startup companies with easier access to potential investors. There may also be some relaxation of the public offering regulations. At this writing, for example, consideration is being given to modifications of Regulation D, an SEC rule that allows some companies to sell securities without registering them with the SEC. This would permit broader marketing and advertising for private offerings to accredited investors.

Fast-Pitch Competitions

The organized angel groups often use "fast pitch" competitions to attract new startup companies that are looking for capital. The competitors in a fast pitch usually make a three or five-minute presentation to an audience of potential investors and other observers.

The idea is an extension of the elevator speech concept. It forces the presenter to describe the essential elements of his business in a very tight and concise format.

Shortly after helping to found the Tech Coast Angels, I attended several fast pitch contests. I got tired of hearing the judges respond with, "You didn't tell me enough about your competition, or market potential, or financial needs." The presenter would usually shrug and say, "But I only had three minutes."

The ability to tell the whole story in three minutes is a very important skill that all entrepreneurs and CEOs should develop. But, as a potential investor, I can't possibly learn enough about a company in three minutes to make an intelligent investment decision, or even to decide if I should spend more time learning about the company. A fast pitch winner might survive a careful due diligence process and get the capital it seeks. But it is also quite possible that the best investment opportunity in the field was not a winner of the fast pitch, because the essential elements of the business could not be compressed into a short slide show.

Shark Tank

Shark Tank is a popular television program in which entrepreneurs present their business concepts to a panel of "sharks," who have the ability to make investments on the spot, if so moved. *Shark Tank* is entertaining both for its interesting product ideas and the look at the sharks and their decision process.

Like the fast pitch competitions, I find *Shark Tank* to be an oversimplified version of how good startup investment deals get done. The sharks ask excellent questions, but the time limits don't allow the audience to see a realistic due diligence process.

For the projects I have seen on *Shark Tank*, the entrepreneur and founder is expected to be the CEO and leader of the company. I'm sure the show has produced some successful companies, but I have observed that the bias for its projects is for the smaller, very entrepreneurial "lifestyle" type businesses in which the entrepreneur makes a good living, but the company is not large enough to provide a good return on a large investment.

Is *Shark Tank* a fast track to a CEO position for the founder or entrepreneur? If the founder receives funding, he may have an opportunity to be the CEO of a startup company, but an inexperienced founder with a small amount of capital doesn't have much advantage over the inexperienced founder without capital. He still doesn't have the skill set of a seasoned CEO.

Advisory Boards

Advisers can be valuable to a company, but they cannot generally provide a fast track to help an inexperienced founder mature. Investors invest in experienced CEOs, not in advisers.

An adviser should be used primarily to make a good CEO even better. Bryon Merade, CEO of Caldera Medical, licensed some medical technology and formed a successful company. Then, after some extensive networking, he recruited a board of experienced directors to help guide the company through its next growth stage. This is an ideal use of advisers. Top CEOs know their weaknesses and surround themselves with experienced advisers as a backstop.

It is important to establish advisory roles in such a way that they do not conflict with the company's board of directors. The decision-making power in a company lies with the board of directors. Establishing a separate "business advisory" group can be counterproductive if it creates conflict with the board. Important business advisers should be on the board of directors so there is no opportunity for conflict.

The best advisory boards are narrowly focused groups of experts that advise on specific issues such as science, technology, manufacturing, or marketing processes. This kind of advisory board can be extremely valuable to a company. If a company creates an advisory board, it should take maximum advantage of the expertise. It should also establish some form of compensation, preferably in the form of stock options, rather than using the company's valuable cash.

Investors often look askance at advisory boards because they know that companies have a tendency to assemble long lists of luminary industry names and then not follow through with them. It is important to arrange periodic meetings and extract real value from an advisory group.

"To Whom Should I Listen?"

Some inexperienced founders think they will be able to succeed by getting advice from a lot of smart people. This is probably a reasonable strategy—if the founder is able to discriminate between people who truly understand what is involved in building a company and those who don't. This is a big if.

Unfortunately, it's very difficult for an inexperienced founder to know to whom to listen for advice. This problem is compounded by the fact that many unqualified people are competing for her attention and funds. These people may be extremely intelligent and well-intentioned, but they may not have the broad range of knowledge and experience required to create a successful startup company. If the wrong adviser is brought in, the founder risks making poor decisions and losing valuable time.

Here are some examples:

- One company with a sporting goods product selected an adviser who had been a successful professional athlete even though he had relatively little business experience.

- A director of a startup company had launched several successful startup companies, but he had no experience with some very important IRS tax regulations. He ran the risk of putting option holders in danger of receiving a big tax bill from the IRS.

- A lead angel investor reviewed a startup company's term sheet, a document outlining an investment, and missed several potentially fatal legal problems.

Who's the best adviser? Let's consider an analogy. If you were having major heart surgery, how would you select a surgeon? Would you select someone who worked in a few hospitals? Someone who observed a few orthopedic surgeries? Someone who watched a few heart surgeries? Someone who just got out of medical school? Someone who performed one successful surgery? Of course not. You'd find the most experienced surgeon who had performed the most heart surgeries, using the most modern technologies, in the most famous hospitals.

If you're looking for advice on how to manage a startup company, you don't go to someone has managed one or two startups or who was a lesser player in a few startups, or a consultant who has never managed a company. You listen to the person in your network who has the most experience in funding and/or managing startup companies.

How About Jumping from a Large Company into a Smaller One?

My summertime work at IBM allowed me to enter Scientific Data Systems at a much higher level than I would have without that experience. The quid pro quo, of course, is that managers in a small company need a broader skill set than those in a large company. And, of course, the CEO of a startup company faces the ultimate challenge, because she needs to be an expert at almost everything. If your experience in the larger companies qualifies you to be the CEO of a smaller one, then, by all means, give it a shot. It might be a good way to accelerate your career.

Conclusion

Looking for a fast track to becoming a successful CEO is a little like trying to become a master chef by reading a few cookbooks, knowing that professional training generally requires a 600-hour course.[2] For those working toward becoming a CEO, there is no substitute for the fifteen to twenty years it takes to acquire the necessary skills.

How do angel investors think about companies? Do they follow the same criteria as venture capitalists, or do they march to a different drummer? We will answer these questions in chapter 11: "Angel Think."

Angel Think

"An angel investor is a person who provides capital, in the form of debt or equity, from his own funds to a private business owned and operated by someone else, who is neither a friend nor a family member."

—Scott A. Shane,
Fool's Gold? The Truth Behind Angel Investing in America

Angelic Motives

Angel investors, as defined by Scott Shane, are not new on the investment scene. Before the 1980s, it was well known that friends and family and so-called angel investors were providing approximately 80 percent of capital to early-stage startup companies. What is relatively new is the proliferation of various *groups* of angel investors, a phenomenon that began in the 1990s. There are key differences, however, between venture capitalists and angel investors, and it is important that the startup company leader understand those differences.

The Angel Concept

The angel groups had an opportunity to fill the vacuum that was created when the best-performing venture capital funds saw their average fund size increase from about $100 million to $500 million and greater, thereby making it almost impossible for them to make "seed" (startup) investments smaller than about $5 million. The concept of the angel group was that it would be possible to raise $500,000 to $1 million on the theory that the average angel's appetite would be about $25,000 per deal. As angel investment has evolved, however, it has become clear that most angel groups do not share the venture capitalists' hunger for disruptive and capital intensive companies. This difference has a profound effect on a startup company's financing strategy.

Tech Coast Angels, One of the Largest Angel Groups

In 1996 Luis Villalobos, the driving force behind Tech Coast Angels, asked me if I would help to form an Orange County angel investment group similar to the Band of Angels in Silicon Valley. I knew Hans Severiens, the founder of the Band of Angels, from attending board meetings at Sierra Semiconductor, where Hans was a director, and I knew a little about his approach to angel investing. I liked the idea of assembling a similar angel investor group in Orange County.

I had learned during my years as a venture capital fund manager that angel investors comprise the bulk of startup company investment. At that time, however, the difficulty in approaching angel investors was that they were hard to find. They were usually contacted one at a time and it would have been a daunting, probably impossible, task to assemble as many as twenty into one investment.

The idea of being able to raise $500,000 to $1 million from approximately 20 angel investors was quite appealing, especially since, by 1997, the venture capital industry had already passed through its "rich-get-richer" phase, leaving a vacuum for smaller seed investments.

Through a series of dinners and follow-up meetings, Luis assembled 10 cofounders for the Orange County chapter of Tech Coast Angels. I agreed, along with six of the other cofounders, to serve on the board of governors, whose initial role was to lay out the operating guidelines for the group's investments.

Getting Organized

One of the fundamental guidelines was that each member would make his own investment decisions and that minimum investments would be $25,000. This meant that, if a startup company wanted to raise capital from the Tech Coast Angels, it needed to persuade at least fifteen–twenty members to invest about $25,000 per person. Each member was responsible for performing his own due diligence. This was done in part to avoid legal complications of having a few members make investment decisions for others. The members were "sophisticated investors," in the legal sense, but they still needed to make their own decisions.

This one operational requirement assured that the investment process would be fairly complicated. There would be a limited number of meetings during which members could do due diligence by questioning a candidate company, but if a member was not completely satisfied after several meetings, he could continue a dialogue with the company in order to get answers important questions.

A second important operational guideline was that each investment opportunity would have one or two member sponsors, or lead investors. If a deal materialized, the sponsors would be responsible for negotiating the investment and structuring the investment documents.

Because of my extensive deal-leading experience as a venture capitalist, I chose to be the sponsor on most of my projects, because I wanted to structure and negotiate deals and provide guidance to the companies.

Only three of my investments were passive, where I was not actively involved. Fortunately, I made a profit on each, because I applied my proven quality standards to the CEO and the management team. Eventually, I found it difficult to lead angel investments, because of the need to assemble about 20 coinvestors, and I saw very few opportunities that satisfied my thirst for disruptive or truly game-changing opportunities with sustainable competitive advantage.

Angelic Ambitions

The initial strategic concept for Tech Coast Angels was that the group would provide companies with seed capital and then to bring in venture capitalists for follow-on capital. This did happen in some deals. However, the follow-on venture capital firms were generally not top-tier. They often did not bring enough capital to ensure the success of the portfolio companies. As this strategy played out in time, the angels became leery of deals requiring follow-on investment by venture capitalists. They worried that the venture capitalists would dilute their percentages of ownership and that their return on investment would be minimal.

My friend, the late Charlie Hobbs, was a primary spokesman for this VC avoidance strategy. Charlie would say, "All we need to do is take companies from a $2 million valuation to a $20 million valuation, and we will have made a very attractive 'ten times' return on investment." Many angel investors say they want a "ten times return" in five years, which is a little less than 60 percent compounded per year. This would be a wonderful result if the angels could obtain it on every investment; unfortunately, the average returns are much lower.

I was not a fan of this strategy. There are not many $2 million companies, especially after the first funding. Many companies are valued in excess of $3 million after their first funding. Further, most companies require more than the initial $1 million or so that an angel group can provide, which means that the angels that start out owning about one-third of the company, perhaps, will probably end up owning one-sixth or less because of the dilution caused by subsequent investments. Finally, I have not seen many successful $20 million exits. So, with respect to Charlie, I do not know of many "two to twenty" deals that have worked out.

My venture capital experience and instincts tell me that you have to swing for the fences in order to have a few big successes in your portfolio, and the angels didn't seem to be taking many full swings.

The need to obtain agreement from twenty or more angels seems to force the angel groups to invest in relatively uncomplicated products and technologies. It is difficult for a group of angel investors to get their minds around highly complex technologies, such as biochemistry, computer chips, or complex big data concepts, for example. In my opinion, this compels them to favor simpler products and business models. Moreover, angel investors are very nervous about having their shareholdings diluted by subsequent investors. This creates a bias in the direction of companies that are not highly capital-intensive.

Putting these two observations together, it seems to me that angels typically steer in a different direction than venture capitalists. They have a preference for simpler technologies and companies that are not likely to need more than a few million dollars in capital to be successful. Obviously, there are exceptions, but this model for angel behavior seems to fit the way they invest more often than not. They rarely follow the venture capitalists' tendency to invest in big, disruptive, and capital-intense companies.

My thinking on angel investment was reinforced substantially when I tried to obtain angel backing for my own startups DRC Computer and NovaDigm Therapeutics. Neither was successful at getting angel capital, but DRC Computer received $7 million in venture capital, and NovaDigm Therapeutics received an $18 million venture capital commitment from Domain Associates, one of the top biotech venture capital funds in the country. In my opinion, the angel model had evolved to a point where it had little tolerance for complicated technology or for capital-intensive projects.

What Color is Your Halo?

It is very difficult to have a successful portfolio without a few home runs, so the angel strategy of bunts and singles, in baseball parlance, is unlikely to work in an overall portfolio mix.

One limitation of some angel investors is that they cannot afford to build a portfolio of thirty or more investments like the venture capitalists. They lean toward a smaller portfolio of less risky deals. Building a portfolio of 10–20 "two to twenty" investments is a bit like playing $5 blackjack in Las Vegas and setting your maximum loss at $100. You can have fun for a while and get a few free drinks, but, in the long term, the casino usually wins.

You would think that angel investors and venture capital investors would think much alike:

- Both are trying to make a return on invested capital.

- Both are dealing with similar risks.

- Both are in a position to provide assistance to their portfolio companies.

The safest assumption to make about angel investors is that they, like venture capitalists, will want qualified CEOs and managers to run their portfolio companies.

It would make sense for angel investors to provide the first capital for companies and then take them to venture capital firms for subsequent financing. But this seems to be the exception, rather than the rule, mostly because the VCs are looking for a different kind of opportunity.

3i Ventures taught me the complexity of making investment decisions in a group framework. When the 3i Ventures team consisted of three or four people, it was relatively easy to make unanimous investment decisions. If we could not reach consensus on a project, we generally did not make the investment. However, when the team size grew to six members, it became clear that we would almost never be able to make a unanimous decision. We changed our policy to making decisions over no more than one "dead body," meaning that a vote of five out of six would represent approval, but a vote of four out of six would not.

If it's that difficult for a VC team of six to make decisions, imagine how difficult it must be within a group of 20 or more independent investors with diverse backgrounds. It's especially challenging to get agreement among 20 investors if the company looking for money has complicated technology or is likely to require substantial additional financing, resulting in dilution, to the early investors.

The Value-Added of Angels

Many angel investors are wealthy because they had an ownership position in one or two very successful companies. But the lessons learned from one or two companies are not necessarily the right lessons for a high-tech startup in a different industry. The best directors usually have broad experience across many different product and market segments, different technologies, different economic conditions, and different fundraising requirements.

Angels often have very strong opinions about business decisions, whereas, in my experience, VCs are more likely to understand that their role is to nudge, coach, encourage, mentor, or guide and otherwise be supportive of management, not to be overly directive. Although, to be fair, the occasional references to "vulture capitalism" are not entirely unfounded.

Angels rarely speak with one voice. In contrast, a venture capital firm is usually represented by a single managing partner in a specific investment. The partnership's recommendations are likely to be well coordinated among the partners. But a company with multiple angel investors will probably receive a lot of advice from different individuals—some of it, conflicting.

Do Angel-Backed Companies Graduate to VC Funding?

It would be reasonable to assume that companies receiving angel financing would naturally progress from angel funding to venture capital funding. It would make sense, for example, for a company to raise $1 million from angel investors, use it to achieve some major milestones thereby increasing value and reducing risk, and then to approach venture capital investors for a larger amount, perhaps in excess of $5 million.

There certainly are companies that have done this. Tech Coast Angels, for example. invested in a company called Green Dot, a provider of prepaid debit cards, which started with angel capital and then raised funds from Sequoia Capital, one of America's top venture capital funds.

However, there often seems to be a disconnect between angel-backed companies and venture capital investments for one or more of the following reasons:

1. Angel investors often lean toward smaller, less capital-intensive companies, rather than more

disruptive "home run" companies that the venture capitalists prefer.

2. Angel investors often steer away from companies that will require additional capital that would dilute their investments.

3. The venture capital funds that coinvest with angels are not always the top-tier funds with deep pockets. These funds have their own deal flow and they generally don't need to see angel deals in order to meet their investment objectives.

4. Some venture capital firms prefer simpler investment structures that do not involve twenty or more angel investors. They may prefer to invest by themselves or to syndicate with one or two other venture capital firms so that only have to listen to a few voices.

It seems that many angel investors follow the advice of a very famous investor:

> ❝ **Never invest in anything you can't illustrate with a crayon.** ❞
>
> —Peter Lynch, *Beating the Street*

Unfortunately, truly disruptive high-tech ideas are often difficult to draw with a crayon.

Conclusion

In his thoughtfully researched book, *Fool's Gold?* Scott A. Shane concludes that angel investors provide capital for a much broader range of companies than venture capitalists. He also concludes that angels' investment returns, overall, are less than venture capitalists and that fewer than 1.5 percent of angel deals result in an IPO or acquisition.[1]

Angel groups can be an important source of capital for startup companies, especially if the company's technology is relatively straightforward, and if future capital requirements are modest. But it is a big mistake to think of the angel groups as venture capitalists willing to do smaller deals. Companies that meet the traditional venture capital criteria of complicated technologies, big and disruptive business models, and significant capital requirements would do well to pursue both angel and venture capital investors in parallel and not put all of their capital eggs in the angel basket.

In chapter 12: "The Solution: Be a Money Magnet," we identify ways to create a fundable startup.

The Solution: Be a Money Magnet

> "The path to success is to make the money come to you."
>
> —Bill Patrianakos, "Making Money Chase You"

Getting the money to chase you is everyone's dream, of course. How can a company make that happen? In this chapter, we present a solution for startups. The most challenging chicken and egg problem facing a startup company is how to get a fundable team without capital and how to get capital without a fundable team. If we can solve this problem, we will be well on our way to creating a successful startup.

So, the challenge is finding a strategy that allows a startup to recruit a founding team and create some value, so that it can take its good idea to investors and have a good chance of attracting capital.

Attracting Capital

The notion of *attracting* capital or being a money magnet is much more relevant to our discussion than the concept of *raising* capital. The process of raising capital implies writing a business plan, knocking on doors, and pounding the pavement. Raising capital suggests that it's a hard sell and that perhaps portions of the proposition may be less than perfect, or missing. For example, the management team may be incomplete. Or the CEO may be underqualified. Or there may not be a credible proof of concept or any created value.

Remember, investors are in the business of searching for good investment opportunities. They are constantly on the lookout for attractive propositions. Presented with a true winner, they are generally more than willing to write a check. The problem is, of course, that most of the opportunities they see are flawed in various ways.

The idea of attracting capital is that if you can resist the temptation to *raise* capital, there may be ways that you can dramatically increase the value of your proposition while reducing risk and greatly enhancing your likelihood of being successfully funded.

The standard reaction to this is, "Yes, but I need money to make anything happen." But do you really? If you apply your creative juices, you might be able to find ways to increase value and reduce risk without capital. Or you might find a way to attract a small amount of capital to in order to meet some short-term objectives. Some of the best startups find a way to build a temporary team, develop a product, get a customer, or develop a prototype without actually raising capital. Then, when these companies do go to the capital markets, they are in a much stronger position with investors, and they have a much higher probability of attracting capital, rather than raising it.

To raise capital, an inexperienced founder will first write a business plan and begin to contact investors. This approach usually suffers from the following problems:

- The team has not been assembled.
- The company does not have a proof of concept or a product.
- The company has no customers.

- Detailed sales and marketing plans have not been developed.

- The company's cash requirements are not well known.

- Professional market and competitive analyses have not been done.

The result, in most cases, is that management approaches investors prematurely and becomes frustrated because the investors are quick to see any weaknesses in the business plan, and they do not see enough value to get excited.

Our interpretation of attracting capital is entirely different. Its basic premise is that professional investors are always on the lookout for attractive investment opportunities. So, the answer is simple: Make them an offer they can't refuse. Create such an attractive investment opportunity that, as word spreads, investors will seek you out. Now you are attracting capital, instead of raising it.

Companies that attract capital do some or all of the following:

- Recruit at least a virtual management team.

- Write a detailed marketing plan and competitive analysis.

- Prepare plausible and achievable revenue and profit forecasts.

- Create a discounted cash flow model of their valuation.

- Develop a product, or at least a working prototype.

- Obtain key strategic partners.

- Get positive feedback from a few beta customers.

Not all companies can make this much progress without capital, but many startups would be surprised at how much value they can create without an infusion of capital. Some of the best managed startups find a way to launch their businesses without raising any outside capital at all. They show investors that they are able to execute their plans. When investors discover a company that has done these things, they are much more likely to invest at a higher valuation.

The first step, of course, is to start with a disruptive, game-changing idea, as described in chapter 1. How do we know that we have a disruptive idea? The founder's first assignment is to make a credible argument that the idea is, in fact, disruptive. This requires the founder to perform extensive market and competitive analysis. Can the company's revenue meet the test of $50 to $100 million in annual sales, or an even higher hurdle for pharmaceutical companies?

Planning a Strategy for Attracting Capital to a Startup

One of the challenges of being a leader is figuring out a sequence of steps that will make the company an attractive investment opportunity. Faced with a bewildering list of tasks that must be completed, experienced company builders can usually find a near-optimal path through the maze. There is no magic-bullet strategy for startup companies to attract capital, but there are some basic principles and essential ingredients that work time after time.

It all starts, of course, with vision—a disruptive concept that appears to solve an important problem in a way that offers an attractive business opportunity. Here are some of the critical steps of the initial strategy for a startup company:

- Articulate the vision.
- Validate the assumptions.
- Measure the market.
- Develop a survival strategy.
- Write the business plan.
- Form the corporation.
- Identify and recruit a founding team.
- Allocate founding shares.
- Build a strong board of directors.
- Implement the plan.
- Create a proof of concept.
- Start the patenting process, if appropriate.
- Take advantage of promising opportunities.
- Find the fundable CEO.
- Compensate the fundable CEO.

These steps do not have to happen in sequence; there may be a lot of overlap. For example, you might identify some additional team members before you finish developing your proof of concept. Here's some further explanation of each of the above activities:

Articulate the Vision

This is never as easy as it sounds. Most inventors are experts in their field. They are extremely knowledgeable about technologies, products, markets, market needs, costs, unsolved problems and so on. They usually have a clear vision of their invention and its opportunities. But describing it so that investors, team members, or corporate partners can understand it can be a challenge. I have watched teams wordsmith documents for months and still not be able to describe a business concept in simple language. But it is important to find a way to explain the idea to a layman; investors do not always understand technical language.

For example, consider Steve Casselman's concept of reconfigurable computing. The concept is simple: it's a computer that can rearrange its internal architecture while processing information. That's a basic definition of reconfigurable computing. But what is the vision? Why would anyone want to build a computer like that? Part of the answer is that it would allow you to do certain tasks in parallel and therefore at a much higher speed. But here is the challenge of describing the vision accurately. How much higher speed? How much faster? How do we know it can be *enough* faster to be exciting? Who would the user be? What would the applications be? How would you create a compiler for such a computer? Exactly how much better is it than existing solutions?

The ultimate answer is that the vision is a computer board that can enable a supercomputer to run 150 times faster at a cost of about $10,000. Now we begin to see the vision in more concrete terms that make it easier to understand how reconfigurable computing can have significant impact on the computing universe. But it took several years of analysis, testing, and benchmarking to arrive at a truly meaningful description.

Validate the Assumptions

Most inventions or business concepts are based on some intuitive assumptions.

- There's a large market.
- The product can be built for a certain cost.
- Customers will buy the product at a specific price.

- Existing vendors do not have a competitive product, and they are not likely to develop one in the future.

- A successful company can be created with a reasonable amount of investment capital, and investors will make an attractive return.

These are typical assumptions, and they are crucial to the success of a company. But in order to attract resources, such as team members, partners, or investors, a startup company must provide some validation of these assumptions.

What does it mean to validate the assumptions? It's not necessary to produce a precise calculation proving each assumption. It's more important to develop a logical and believable estimate. For example, an estimate of the potential number of buyers for a product might be obtained by calculating the current number of users or the number of people in the world who have a specific problem. For a vaccination against hospital-acquired infections, an estimate of the number of customers might be the number of patients to enter a hospital every year for major surgery. For a reconfigurable computer, it might be the number of people using supercomputers.

Once the number of potential buyers has been estimated it is fairly simple to estimate the percentage of potential buyers who might actually make a purchase each year. This number multiplied by the expected price of the product yields an estimate for annual potential revenue. Our purpose here is not to explain how to do market forecasting. It is fairly simple to develop a logical and defensible guesstimate revenue forecast. Other factors, such as the size of the existing industry, or existing competitors, can be incorporated to support the estimate. When developing these estimates, it's more important to be roughly right than to be precisely wrong. Plausibility and achievability trump precision.

Measure the Market

Usually, it is possible to get a reasonable estimate with a relatively simple, intuitive thought process. How many people are buying similar products today? How much better is your product? How many people might buy your product? How many people have the problem you propose to solve? How quickly will the market develop? Will there be a long trial period, during which only early innovators and thought leaders will buy the product? Or will the benefits be obvious and compelling, leading to early and rapidly growing sales? At what price can the product be sold? Is there an existing point of comparison? Is there a similar product in the market today? At what price? Is a solution to the problem available today? At what price?

By answering questions like these, the founder or inventor should be able to arrive at a logical and defensible projection for revenues for the product during the first few years of sales. If the forecast is less than $50 million in sales by the fifth year, investors may question whether or not the company has a truly disruptive idea. If the fifth-year forecast exceeds $50 million in sales, or, even better, $100 million in sales, the founder may have an attentive audience.

Computer Aided Design Group (CADG) developed a very sophisticated computer program for managing the assets of a corporation in very detailed and dynamic ways. It was an extremely powerful system, and it seemed that it would benefit any corporation with more than one location. But, on close analysis, it turned out that only a few Fortune 100-sized companies could cost-justify use of the system. It was not cost-effective for smaller companies, which limited the potential market size.

Develop a Survival Strategy

Every company should have a survival strategy. What if the company is not able to raise capital? How far can the company go without capital? The answer for some companies is not very far. But many startup companies could build a skeleton management team without capital. And, using this skeleton team, a company might be able to build a prototype product and obtain a few customers. Having done this, the company might be able to attract a CEO capable of raising venture capital, or angel funds.

But a majority of startup companies pursue the opposite strategy. They write a business plan and immediately start approaching investors. And then they are puzzled when investors ask questions like, "What experience does your team have? What experience does your CEO have? When will you have a working prototype? When will you have your first customer?" This approach is a recipe for failure in raising initial capital, or in raising insufficient capital, so that the company operates for a few months and then needs more money, but without having accomplished any milestones that would justify additional investment at a higher valuation.

The goal of the survival strategy, then, is to find a way to move the company forward without raising money, or at least without raising a significant amount. Generally, this means proving the basic concept, developing a working prototype product, or developing a product that can be sold. The survival plan answers the question, "What is involved in completing these tasks and what people will be required to complete them?"

At this stage, the primary resources the company will need are most likely product design and development people. But it is extremely important at this stage that the design process be firmly rooted in sound information about the requirements for the product. It is important to get as much customer feedback as possible. Some companies perform focus group interviews in order to get this information. Others simply discuss the project with potential customers. Some build a working product and invite several customers to be a beta test site (testing a prerelease version of the product) for purposes of validating the product concept.

One of the first questions the team must address is how far it can go without capital. There are several reasons for focusing on this question:

- It may be impossible for the team to raise capital at the outset, so they must decide if they can accomplish anything meaningful without raising money.

- There is value in moving a company as far forward as possible without raising capital. A company improves its chances of raising capital as it achieves more milestones by strengthening the team or advancing the technology, for example.

- These accomplishments also reduce the risk to investors, which is another way of helping the company obtain a higher valuation.

- A bootstrapping strategy may be necessary if the company has trouble raising money. A company should always have a survival strategy to help it stay alive if it is unable to raise capital, or if it takes longer than expected to raise capital. This is true at every stage of the company's development.

The idea of operating without capital is abhorrent to most founders and understandably so. It would not be anyone's first choice, and, for some companies, it may not be possible. This might suggest other strategies, such as looking for a partner who can provide the capital equipment. But in my experience most companies are too quick to assume that they need money. Often, the best startups are the ones that achieve a lot of milestones with no infusion of capital. They adopt a lean and mean approach to running the business, which is extremely healthy. It gives prospective investors confidence that their money will be managed responsibly.

Write the Business Plan

A startup needs a well-articulated strategic plan and operating plan in order to make sure the team understands the company's objectives and how they are to be met. The best vehicle for creating and documenting this kind of plan is a document that can later become a slide presentation for investors, and I recommend using PowerPoint or a similar slide format. On each slide, write simple bulleted phrases, which minimizes the amount of writing to be done and in most cases improves your audience's comprehension. These bullet points can be expanded hierarchically to include a lot of detail in as few words as possible. Slides can be re-arranged by simply "dragging" to change the order. In my experience, the same document written as 30 pages of text would take much longer for an audience to understand, and changes require tedious cutting and pasting.

Working in PowerPoint, your fifty-slide business plan can be easily distilled into a compelling presentation of fifteen to twenty slides for investors. The longer plan still provides more detail and a framework for the management team to discuss important topics fully. Internal communication is greatly improved by using the PowerPoint format.

Guides, outlines, and templates for creating a business plan are readily available online or at the bookstore. Unfortunately, most writers simply fill in the blanks in an outline with the minimum information. For example, they might list the members of their management team or perhaps even each manager's past positions. But this does not provide the information that an investor really wants: why this management team is best suited to build this company at this time and in this industry.

Here is another example of how using a standard business plan guide won't guarantee that you will give investors the information they really need. When the guide asks you to specify who your competition is, most companies list their competitors and possibly write down some of their own company's advantages. But the question an investor wants answered is, "What are the dynamics of competition within your industry? Who are the existing vendors, and on what basis do they compete? What are the most important competitive criteria? Pricing? Performance? Product size? Response time? Power requirements? How do the existing vendors attempt to gain competitive advantage?"

Planning is a vitally important discipline. Yet, surprisingly, I meet many executives who don't believe in planning. Their attitude is, "I can't predict the future, so why write a plan?"

The purpose of a plan is not to predict the future rather it is to make sure that the team is communicating effectively about what it wants to accomplish and that it has a rationale and agreement for its actions. It takes considerable time to develop a good plan. One of the most useful courses I took as an undergraduate student at Ohio Wesleyan University was a class in business letter writing, taught by Professor Libby Reed.

In the class, I learned how to write many different kinds of business letters, some of them difficult, such as job rejection letters, credit refusals, and sales turndowns. The lessons learned in that class have served me extremely well. Much of my time is spent helping companies make their written plans more clear. It is important, of course, to develop the right strategies and business models. But if you have the best strategies and business models and don't articulate them clearly, you've lost the battle.

Form the Corporation

A founder needs to form a legal entity and get it authorized in order to open a bank account and hire employees. I've seen many founders perseverate over questions like, "Should we be a C corporation? Should we be an S corporation? Should we be an LLC?" The best advice regarding questions like these is that you should talk to a lawyer. An experienced corporate lawyer can resolve these issues quickly. But inexperienced founders, for some reason, are often reluctant to talk to lawyers.

One of the worst mistakes a founder can make is to try to play lawyer. Yes, lawyers can be expensive. You need to find one that is reasonably priced. I've been blessed by having a lawyer partner who is willing to do some of the fundamental organizational work for a small percentage of the company's stock.

An experienced founder working with a qualified corporate lawyer will create a shareholders' agreement for her company. This document is an agreement among the founding shareholders. It defines the company's business, and it deals with potentially knotty issues like, "What if someone stops doing his job? What if a founder competes with the company? Who owns technology developed by the founders or other employees?" Any one of these questions, left open and unaddressed, can cause very serious problems for a startup.

Identify and Recruit a Founding Team

Ideally, the early team would implement the first major milestone, whether it is a theoretical proof of concept, a working prototype, or an actual working product. A virtual team often comprises part-time members who are compensated with stock instead of cash. Their mission is usually to create an initial product or perform some other task critical to launching the startup company.

Once the necessary skills have been identified, the founder builds a virtual management team. To do this, he offers each member an appropriate percentage of the company's equity. Determining these percentages can seem like guesswork, but I personally have used a spreadsheet approach to allocate founders' shares based on past contributions, present contributions, and expected future contributions of each team member.

The need to identify the initial team drives everything else:

- What needs to happen?
- What help do you need?
- How do you assemble a team?
- How do you compensate the team?

Inventors often have colleagues who can add value to the initial efforts of a startup company. It's important to think through what skills will be required and when, and what skills will be needed to complement those of the founder. Building the initial team is one of the many chicken and egg problems a startup will face. It is difficult to get team members without capital, and it's difficult to get capital without a team.

In order to work through these kinds of problems, a leader must adopt the attitude that there is no such thing as a dilemma. All problems are solvable. The solution to most chicken and egg problems is to take some tiny little "chicken" steps and some tiny little "egg" steps until there is a breakthrough.

In the case of assembling and compensating a team, some tiny but effective steps can be asking people to work part time (part of the chicken) in exchange for founder's stock (part of the egg).

Allocate Founding Shares

The capitalization plan for founders is a distribution of the initial shares of the corporation among the founders. While it may be tempting to distribute shares equally, or on the basis of personal friendships, it is extremely important that founders' shares be allocated in proportion to the value of their past, present, and estimated future contributions.

Team members will vary in their ability to work for stock instead of salary. The idea is to compensate them for part-time contributions during the startup stages and before the company can afford to pay salaries.

I like to use a spreadsheet that allows me to rank each person's past, present and expected future contributions. This allows me to adjust the weighting between past contributions and future contributions. While past contributions are important and should be rewarded, future contributions should be weighted more heavily as they will determine the success or failure of the company. They are likely to create most of the value the company obtains upon exit.

This task often confuses first-time founders. Many assume that the company's technology has enormous intrinsic value. The problem with this thinking is that technology does not commercialize itself. While the underlying science and patents may be extremely valuable, they are worthless without the years of hard work by qualified leaders and managers, who will need to be compensated at competitive market rates.

Although working with this spreadsheet method may seem a little simplistic, it allows a founding team to be thoughtful about allocating shares to past, present and future contributors. Is there a better way? Probably, but this basic approach is more rational than the process most startups use.

Build a Strong Board of Directors

By far the most common reason I hear for recruiting a member of the board of directors of a startup company is that the candidate has great industry contacts. Let's discuss the logic of this as a reason for recruiting a director.

First, let's agree that having a lot of contacts within an industry is a good thing. But there are some issues that need to be explored. The first concern, of course, is what is the company trying to accomplish? Is it trying to sell a product?" If so, it needs contact with buyers. Is it trying to enter into a corporate strategic partnership? Then it needs high-level contacts. Does it need to subcontract manufacturing? If it is, it needs contacts within manufacturing organizations. Is it trying to subcontract engineering work? If so, it will seek out contacts within engineering organizations. An executive might have a lot of industry contacts, but are they the specific contacts that are needed to meet the company's objectives?

Second, how strong a relationship does the executive have with her contacts? Are they casual acquaintances? Or can she still call her contacts and ask for important information?

Finally—and this may be the most challenging question—how current are the executive's contacts? One Bureau of Labor Statistics study showed that employees between the ages of 18 and 44 had changed jobs an average of 11 times, or every 2.3 years, on average, for the older employees.[1] This means that an employee's closest contacts change every few years. In my experience an executive's Rolodex has a half-life of two to three years, meaning that about half of the contacts become obsolete during that period. If an executive's active relationship with a specific person was two years ago, there's a good chance that the contact is now either in a different position or with a different company.

Therefore, the strategy of recruiting based on strong industry contacts is rarely effective. I have served on a number of boards where a director was sought after because of his high-level industry contacts. But, when the startup company needed help on a specific issue, the director's response was almost always something like, "Well, it's been a while since I've worked with him; he's in a different position; or he's changed companies."

In fairness, I do think there's enormous value in having directors who understand how a particular industry works. This is not the same as having live contacts within the industry. Every industry has its own peculiarities when it comes to selling, marketing, public relations, and strategic partnerships. It is important to have executives and directors who understand how an industry works, but I believe that the most overriding skill a director should have is the knowledge of how to build a company within that industry.

It is important to assemble a board of directors with balanced skills. If the CEO has any functional areas of weakness, such as accounting, sales, manufacturing, marketing, or business development, it is important to try to backstop his weakness with a board member who is strong in that function.

Many boards of directors have five people. Once a company has obtained capital, it's fairly common that the CEO is the only member of management serving on the board. Other directors might be investors, industry experts, or people who have extensive experience at building companies. The most important responsibility of a director of a high-tech company is to decide if the CEO is meeting the company's objectives and should remain in her position. A board's primary remedy, if things are not going well, is to replace the CEO, which occurred in six out of twelve of my venture capital portfolio companies.

Implement the Plan

This approach to launching a startup involves many moving parts. It underscores the need for experienced leadership because of the following challenges:

- Team members are often part-time participants that have other work assignments and conflicts.

- Working without salary or cash compensation can create stress for team members.

- Coordinating and effectively managing a virtual team requires strong management skills.

- Even though the company has no capital, it is functioning like a funded company with a management team, well-developed plans and objectives, frequent team meetings, and tight schedules.

Developing and implementing plans for such a virtual operation requires significant executive skills.

Create a Proof of Concept

Proof of concept is a kind of shorthand for, "Show me that it works." Investors and potential strategic partners do not like to take the risk of product invention, so it's important for them to see some objective demonstration that the product does or can work. The validation does not necessarily have to be an actual working product. It might be a working prototype, a simulation model, a mathematical proof, or, in the case of a drug, proof that it works in animals or in a test tube. There is lots of room here to be creative. Investors and partners are willing to listen to any feasible argument that the product is well-conceived and that it can be developed without a significant amount invention. The key is to demonstrate that completion of the product will not involve a never-ending process of innovation.

Start the Patenting Process, If Appropriate

Patenting your idea can be difficult if your company has no capital. Patents are not cheap. But one potentially lifesaving mechanism is the provisional patent, which allows a company to reserve a filing date for its application. If you think your technology is patentable, you should find a way to have at least an exploratory conversation with a patent attorney, if only to understand your future options.

Take Advantage of Promising Opportunities

It's important for startup companies to balance anecdotal opportunity (one-at-a-time) with a systematic approach (exploring multiple alternatives). Opportunities appear unexpectedly, and it is incumbent on a startup company's management to pursue them with diligence. On the other hand, the company's best candidate for CEO or VP of sales may not be the guy who lives next door. Some companies fail because they take the easy way out in solving problems. They jump at the first opportunity.

One company, for example, chose a CEO whose only management experience was that of director of engineering. He just happened to be the only business executive that the founder knew. This kind of anecdotal hiring is usually a mistake. Successful companies typically go through a more systematic process of defining the job requirements, writing a job description, and doing extensive networking in search of candidates. The ideal solution of course would be to retain an executive recruiting firm but here we are again up against the chicken and egg problem. How do we retain an executive search firm without cash? A few executive recruiters might work for stock instead of fees, but they are rare.

Find the Fundable CEO

Every startup's goal should be to find a CEO who will excite venture capitalists and help it raise the capital it needs.

Finding a fundable CEO can be tricky. The challenge is that when a company has no committed capital it is extremely difficult to recruit a top-flight CEO. Like most people, CEOs like to be paid. An unfunded company might attract a CEO who is desperate for a first assignment, but a highly qualified CEO is likely to join an unfunded company only under very special circumstances.

A highly qualified CEO does not need to take a job in an unfunded company. He is probably getting offers from well-funded companies. Furthermore, the CEO who would accept a job in an unfunded company is probably not the best candidate.

The best time to recruit a CEO is after a company has received financing. This way, the company can compete with other funded companies for top CEO talent.

From the CEO's point of view, the obvious advantage is that he does not have to take the risk that he might not succeed in raising capital for your company. When an unfunded company recruits a CEO, it is expecting the CEO to help raise capital, which means that that person might end up as the CEO of a company without capital to pay his salary for an extended period of time.

Another reason that a funded company has a significant advantage in hiring a CEO is that it probably has the resources to relocate a CEO from anywhere in the country, or even in the world. A startup company without money is most likely limited to hiring a CEO who already lives nearby.

Hiring a CEO for an unfunded company is doable, but it is not easy. The key is to find a CEO who:

- Has been successful in the past.

- Lives nearby.

- Is able to work for a period of time without a salary.

- Is seeking a significant equity opportunity.

- Has finished an assignment and is looking for a new company. For example, he might have been replaced, or he might have sold his previous company.

Some successful managers in large companies do not feel that they have enough stock to create substantial wealth, so they decide to move to a smaller company in exchange for significant equity.

It's important to not hire a CEO out of desperation because of a lack of capital, only to find out that he is not the right person for the job. The main protection against this is to check the references of any CEO candidate thoroughly before making any hiring decision. The founder and the board of directors should call all of the references supplied and they should identify some references of their own through their own networks of contacts so they have references other than those provided by the candidate. The references provided by the candidate should be called, but the safe assumption is that they were given because they are friends. These references are less likely to give negative feedback than independent references discovered by the hiring party.

How do you find your dream CEO? Your best tool is aggressive networking. The more value you've created, the better. CEOs are like investors; they are always looking for good opportunities. Here are the keys to finding the right CEO for your company:

- Use your virtual team to create as much value as possible in order to attract the attention of a CEO in search of an opportunity.
- Spread the word, through aggressive networking, that you are looking for a CEO. Network with as many CEOs, entrepreneurs, and investors as you can.
- Polish your recruiting elevator speech and make sure lots of people have a clear understanding of your vision, mission, and plans.
- Mobilize your personal network to help with the search.

Startup companies usually don't have the resources to retain an executive recruiter, but you should still talk to every recruiter you can find, in the hope that one might do a favor for a CEO in their files in order to do some relationship building.

Compensate the Fundable CEO

Forget about the multimillion dollar annual salaries you read about in the press. Qualified startup CEOs know that their companies cannot afford such astronomical compensation. But, remember, we're going after a well-qualified CEO, who won't be inexpensive.

Most startup CEOs receive annual salary and bonus in the range of $80,000–300,000, depending on the size, stage, and funding of the company. Their equity percentage is often in the range of 4 to 6 percent, again, depending on the size, stage, and funding of the company.

A fundable CEO who joins a startup early enough to be considered a cofounder may command a much higher percentage, depending on the number of founders. It would not be unusual for a founding CEO to receive more than 15 percent of a company's equity.

Don't make the mistake that many founders make by cutting off their nose to spite their face. They decide that a certain amount of equity is too much to give up for a CEO, or for funding. They often end up killing their company because they do not capture the management and capital they need to be successful.

The CEO and management team are necessary ingredients of a startup. It's impossible to be successful without them. How much should you pay for an indispensable ingredient? How much would you pay for chocolate if you're making a chocolate cake? Ultimately, you must do what you have to do to be successful. There are no absolutes that define too much or too little. Many successful entrepreneurs have given away a big piece in order to bake the cake.

Go Get the Money

Conventional wisdom holds that a company seeking the attention of a venture capital firm needs a referral. It is probably best to approach a venture capitalist with an introduction from a lawyer, accountant, or other service provider, if possible. However, it is important to remember that venture capitalists are paid for making good investments, so they don't just sit back and wait for deals to appear. On the contrary, they network aggressively in the high-tech community to find good investment opportunities. They research new technologies in order to identify promising startups. They go to conferences to stay abreast of competitive trends in multiple markets. They scour universities for technologies that have the potential to be turned into exciting products.

> When I managed 3i Ventures, I assumed that the best deal we would ever see would come "across the transom," rather than through a referral. We were happy to look at any investment opportunity that appeared viable. Most of our deals were referrals, but a significant percentage of our support went to companies that simply contacted us and asked us to review their business plans. Some investments were made proactively, because we identified a promising technology and sought out one of the leading developers.

Communicating Clearly

Clear communication is essential during the startup and fundraising process. This means clear communication and mutual understanding between and among the founders, the CEO, and investors or potential corporate partners. This is obvious and it probably sounds trite, but it operates at a level well beyond most people's understanding of what clear communication means. Here's an example that illustrates its importance and why it is critical to pay attention to it.

In 2010 the cofounders of PulSentry, Inc. wrote an application for an NIH Small Business Innovation Research (SBIR) grant. The grant received a poor review, so we spent a number of months trying to clean up the document. As we proceeded, we realized that the document contained many internal inconsistencies. This was due, in part, to the complex structure of the grant application. The request for information often asks the same question in slightly different ways, so that it is easy to end up with extensive duplication. For this reason, we decided that instead of rewriting the grant application we would produce a very structured white paper that would state each important point only once, thereby minimizing the opportunity for duplication and inconsistencies caused by saying the same thing in slightly different ways. Our plan was to create the white paper and then cut and paste it into a grant format for the next submission of our application.

Working several hours a week on this clean-up process, it took us months to write the new document. This sounds like an enormous amount of time to write a sixteen-page document, and it is. However most of the time was not spent spinning our wheels and wordsmithing. The time-consuming challenge was the process of unscrambling the internal inconsistencies, making substantive additions to the strategy, and thinking through numerous complicated medical and technical issues.

PulSentry's product deals with the early detection of a medical condition called cardiac tamponade. In carefully reviewing our document, we discovered that there were conflicting references to the importance of *timing* in detecting cardiac tamponade before it becomes fatal. In order to communicate clearly the efficacy of our product, the team had to make those references consistent, and this process involved a group of fairly skilled authors who have published many papers and books.

We felt that this single issue could make the difference between acceptance or rejection of our grant application. It is a good example of the effort that is required in a business plan presentation in order to send a clear message to investors.

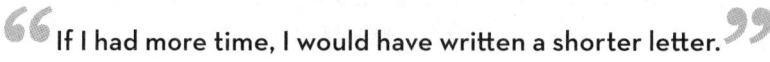

If I had more time, I would have written a shorter letter.

—Mark Twain

Mark Twain's famous quotation may be a shortened version of a similar sentiment.

«Je n'ai fait celle-ci plus longue que parce que je n'ai pas eu le loisir de la faire plus courte.»[2]

(*Rough translation:* "I made this longer because I didn't have time to make it shorter.")

—Blaise Pascal

In any case, it takes lots of time to write a compact, concise and effective business plan.

In the rest of this chapter, I'll present two examples of companies that did a good job of attracting capital, some thoughtful questions from Van Honeycutt (See interview in chapter 9) about recruiting a CEO for a startup company, and a model for spinning companies out of a technology laboratory:

- Shy Pahlevani and LiveSafe, Inc.
- Dr. Jack Edwards and NovaDigm Therapeutics, Inc.
- Van Honeycutt on importing a CEO
- Technology spinouts at their best: The Langer Lab at MIT

CASE STUDY

Shy Pahlevani and Building the LiveSafe (Formerly CrimePush) Team

Shy Pahlevani's dream had its genesis in a very unpleasant situation. Shy was robbed at gunpoint on Capitol Hill, in Washington, DC. His immediate thought was that there should be a way to use his cell phone, not just to call 911 but to send video or text or images directly to law enforcement personnel.

At the time, people often used their smart phone to take a video, still photograph, or audio recording of a crime, but their only option was to post it on a social media website like Twitter or FaceBook. Shy thought there should be a way for people to communicate crime information directly to law enforcement agencies like the local 911 operator or a college campus security office.

Shy conceived a mobile app for doing this, and he set out to build a company. His attitude was, "I don't want to keep this a secret. I need to share my idea with as many people as possible." Every time he spoke to someone about his product, he asked himself, "How can this person help build the company?" At that time, Shy had only one cofounder, his brother, Eman, and no capital with which to fund the startup.

Building the Virtual Team

Below, in the words of Shy Pahlevani, founder of LiveSafe (formerly CrimePush), is a description of how he created the founding team and bootstrapped LiveSafe to a level where it could acquire both more seasoned managers and capital:

Building a startup team is all about timing. You can't hire the most seasoned people at the beginning. But you want to control your own destiny and make your vision a reality.

It's actually difficult to hire employees even in their thirties when you're compensating them with stock and not cash. In our first year, we just wanted to build the initial product. We didn't need a lot of senior executives. All of our initial team members were in their 20s.

Here's the sequence in which our initial team was built.

1. *I was employee number one. My role was to orchestrate the startup process.*

2. *My brother Eman was employee number two. He focused on strategic partnerships and early sales.*

3. *Our third team member was a developer who created an Apple version of our app. This was the easiest way to get started, and it got us in front of early adopters.*

4. *After several months Samir joined us as employee number four to help with marketing and improving the aesthetics of our website.*

5. *During this early process everyone had to wear a lot of hats. We all had to do just about everything.*

6. *Our fifth employee was another designer whose task was to polish the website and product and make them more user friendly.*

7. *Over the next few months we had several developers and designers come and go. A few of them didn't work out. A few did and stayed.*

That initial team made enough progress that we were able to begin, with the help of several senior advisers (including myself), to talk to investors. Once we got some

initial funding, we added a product manager, two addi-
tional developers, and a salesperson. We got some great
early PR because the police chiefs who bought our prod-
uct got excited about it and helped us get in front of
local media, including TV stations.

Once we raised our initial angel round of $1.5 million,
we were able to attract a CEO and chairman. We had
to find the right person to work with our staff of young
people. Since then we have had two additional rounds
of funding, and now the challenge is, 'how fast can we
grow?'

This process motivated and united team members, got people interested in the idea, and helped the company build momentum.

Getting to Product

During its first year, LiveSafe had no product, no customers, and no cash, but Shy's unique process helped create crucial momentum. The virtual team used email updates to schedule upcoming meetings, to notify people about meetings with customers or potential partners, new contracts, the overall roadmap, status of product development, and progress in obtaining initial customers. The team still celebrates every new deal by email. The process has become part of the culture.

The next step was to quantify and describe the opportunity in detail. This involved gathering extensive data on the number of law enforcement agencies and campus security offices. The company has discovered that campus security offices are often very receptive to its marketing message. Its current strategy is to sell to police departments, university security offices, and corporations.

Early Customers

One of LiveSafe's best customers is the University of Southern Califoria (USC). USC students had a strong cultural aversion to communicating with campus security, even though there was at least one situation where appropriate communication might have saved a life. Today, 46 percent of USC students have adopted the application. LiveSafe now has fourteen university campus clients in California, its second best state for customers. The top state is Virginia, where 80 percent of the universities are LiveSafe clients.

From the beginning, LiveSafe received flattering media attention. Network television programs often approached LiveSafe for interviews, because they were contacted about LiveSave's successes. For a short time, the company paid a public relations representative for getting media interviews. However, as the company began to add more universities as clients, it found that the universities were glad to publicize their adoption of the app, and LiveSafe benefitted from the publicity.

During the process of creating the virtual team, Shy was very aware of the potential pothole of recruiting the wrong people to the team. He did have a few false starts, but he was quick to ask people to leave if he felt they were not making an adequate contribution.

The primary objective of the virtual team was to develop a prototype product and get at least one beta customer. Recognizing the need to provide an incentive to his team, Shy began to offer equity as a form of compensation.

Getting Attention and Seed Capital

LiveSafe has one competitor: a product called Rave, that has received about $70 million in venture capital. Shy believes that LiveSafe's competitive advantage derives from its ability to market its products and implement customer sites effectively.

LiveSafe is fortunate to be among the only 1 percent of all mobile apps that have received over 100,000 downloads. Its primary focus, today, is on marketing to colleges, universities, and corporations.

When the company needed some additional initial capital, Shy appealed to friends, family, and a few members of the virtual team. He easily assembled about $100,000. Getting those funds was critical to moving to the next stage.

One member of the virtual team, Jeff Grass, had managed several venture-backed companies. He spoke at one of Shy's business school classes and he later hired Shy as an intern for one of his companies. Jeff was running another company, but he began to provide some capital to LiveSafe and he took over the reins as CEO once his other project was completed.

With help from Jeff and the business plan presentation we created, LiveSafe was able to raise about $1.5 million in capital from angel and small investor groups. About one year later, IAC, Barry Diller's (chairman and senior executive of IAC/InterActiveCorp and Expedia, Inc.) venture capital firm, invested approximately $6.5 million in the company.

Next Time?

Shy works closely with Jeff, and he sees himself as gradually learning the skills required to eventually become a CEO. He recognizes that a good CEO must excel at 30 to 40 critical business skills (see the list in chapter 8), and he believes he is gradually mastering them. He has dreams of becoming a fundable CEO, and he is pursuing his goal in a sensible way.

(From my interview with Shayan Pahlevani, Founder LiveSafe, Inc.,
December 1, 2015.)

Van Honeycutt on Importing a CEO

During our interview on November 15, 2015 (see chapter 9), Van Honeycutt, Former Chairman and CEO of Computer Science Corporation, had some questions about the strategy of recruiting experienced CEOs for startups, and his concerns are worth noting. Van's right, "It ain't always easy."

The first question Van asked is, "Isn't it difficult to unplug a CEO from a company midstream to run a startup?" Absolutely. If a CEO is gainfully employed, performing well, enjoying his assignment, and attractively compensated, there is not much reason for him to leave that for a startup company. In almost all of cases I have observed, the CEO who moved to a startup was—or was about to be—in between assignments. At any one moment in time, there will be some CEOs "in the float," either unemployed or dissatisfied to the point that they will be open to considering a new assignment. I can envision a situation where a large-company CEO feels that he could obtain more wealth by moving to a startup, because large-company compensation is usually based on relatively large salaries, but relatively little stock ownership. But I don't know that this happens frequently. Finally, I am reminded of Bill White's remark, "My job is to pull people out of large companies and put them in small ones." Most of the movement of executives is in the direction of smaller firms where they can have more responsibility and greater equity compensation.

Van's second question is, "Aren't most founders going to be too impatient to work with an imported CEO?" My answer was, "Yes, some will be, but if they don't get over it, they'll probably fail." Picking the right CEO for a startup is not easy. The CEO and the founder must form a strong partnership. Look back at Steve Casselman's comments about bringing Larry Laurich in as CEO, and you will see some of the issues that arose in their relationship, for better and for worse. The founder and CEO should have a written agreement that describes their working relationship and spells out the responsibilities for each.

Van's third question is, "Doesn't a CEO have to 'own' her product?" Yes, ownership is important, but the CEO doesn't have to be the inventor. In the case studies of DRC, NovaDigm, Live-Safe, and Boost Academy, the incoming CEO did extensive due diligence—about the same level of due diligence a venture capitalist would do. In three of the cases, the CEO did, in fact, make an investment in the company. These CEOs knew what they were getting into. They dug into the technology, and they checked markets and competition very carefully. After all, they were making significant personal commitments to these companies. So, yes, it's important for the CEO to own the technology and product. But a knowledgeable and smart CEO with at least some technological capacity can do her own extensive due diligence in order to buy into the company's concept. Experienced CEOs are usually quick studies.

Spinout Companies

One form of startup company is the "spinout" company formed around technology from a university or research institute. Spinouts are an important part of the process known as technology transfer or technology commercialization.

The Tech Transfer Spinout Company

The process of commercializing technology can involve, when justified by economic considerations, creating a spinout company. This is the best way to gather the resources required to build value and capitalize on the inherent value of the technology.

Academic and research institutions create an enormous amount of *potentially* valuable technology. Many measure their success by the number of patents in their portfolio. Others try to derive revenue from their patent portfolio by engaging in various out-licensing activities. Some patents have created enormous royalty revenue for the institutions where they were invented. But, in my experience, the big bucks are more likely to come from spinout companies constructed around technologies. Few technology transfer organizations have the machinery to create spinouts, however.

The inventors of a technology are often the most qualified people to develop it into a product. This doesn't mean that they should necessarily lead the effort. It just suggests that they may need to be involved to make the project successful.

Why would this be true?

Many of the most promising technologies are complicated. The reason they got invented in the first place was that the concepts were not obvious or easy to understand. In many cases they are the result of years of research, exploration, and experimentation. Handing off a complicated technology to a company that does not have a thorough grounding in it, or to a team of individuals who have not been involved from the beginning, often does not work.

For a significant percentage of new technologies—at least the ones with substantial promise—the best way to extract value from them is to build a spinout company involving the inventors.

In my opinion, this is where most tech transfer organizations come up short. They rarely have the ability to create spinout companies, because they don't have people on their staffs who are experienced at creating successful new startup companies.

The Langer Lab at MIT, named for Professor Robert Langer, illustrates how value is created when a team of knowledgeable inventors create a spinout company with the help of experienced and effective company builders.

CASE STUDY

Making Spinouts Work: The Langer Lab at MIT

Robert Langer's lab at MIT is one of the most prolific sources of spin-out companies in the United States. Since the 1980s, it has produced over twenty-five spinout companies, some of which have been extremely successful.[3] You would think the lab should be a model for technology transfer across the United States. It should be. But it's success is a function of a rather unique circumstance.

The Langer Lab comprises fifty-seven researchers in a relatively narrow space—tissue engineering, drug delivery, medical devices, drug development, and cell engineering.[4] Robert Langer, the lab director, has a close working relationship with Terry McGuire, a partner at the Polaris Partners venture capital fund.[5] Polaris Partners is a $4 Billion venture capital fund with an office in nearby Boston. Polaris Partners manages over $4 Billion in capital through five "funds." The fifth fund, Polaris V, is a $1 Billion fund. In addition to its Managing Partners, Polaris has employees who help companies write business plans, research markets and competition, build management teams, negotiate corporate deals and raise capital.[6]

Terry McGuire has been the driving "company building" force behind the companies that have spun out of the Langer Lab. When Terry McGuire sees a technology with commercial potential, he and some of Polaris's staff perform the business fundamentals.[7]

They write the business plan; they perform market and competitive analysis; they recruit the management team. They provide the experienced business expertise required to successfully launch a new spinout company.

This approach is Ideal. It provides the leadership required to build successful companies, and it has been proven many times. It puts the business responsibility In the hands of experts who select the "fundable idea" and recruit the "fundable management team."

If every tech transfer office had a Terry McGuire and some appropriate support resources, the number of successful tech transfer spin outs would skyrocket.

Most institutions do not have the machinery in place to create and nurture successful spinouts. Some have created "incubators" and some may have "mentoring" staffs for the founders of these companies. But all eventually bump into the same problem: Unless a startup company has an experienced leader as a founder, it is unlikely to be highly successful. Incubators and mentors cannot provide the leadership required. Investors do not invest in incubators and mentors. They invest in capable management teams. The company will be as strong as its CEO and his team and his previous experience.

This approach is Ideal. It provides the leadership required to build a successful company, and it has been proven many times. It puts the business responsibility in the hands of experts who select the fundable idea and recruit the fundable management team.

If every tech transfer office had a Terry McGuire and some appropriate support resources, the number of successful tech transfer spinouts would skyrocket.

Most institutions do not have the machinery in place to create and nurture successful spinouts. Some have created incubators and some may have mentoring staffs for the founders of these companies. But all eventually bump into the same problem: Unless a startup company has an experienced leader as a founder, it is unlikely to be highly successful. Incubators and mentors cannot provide the leadership required. Investors do not invest in incubators and mentors. They invest in capable management teams.

The company will be as strong as its CEO and his team and his previous experience.

In order to extract value from a patent, it is often necessary to add value in the form of proof of concept, market analysis, or competitive analysis. While not all patents have enough commercial potential to justify creation of a new company, most technology transfer organizations would be well served to develop a spinout-friendly culture. That is, a culture that encourages the inventors and holders of the patents to partner with business leaders who are capable of creating a new company, based on the technology, that can attract the necessary investment capital.

CASE STUDY

At NovaDigm Therapeutics, Inc. Dr. Jack Edwards fulfills his dream of testing a Candida vaccine in human patients

Dr. Jack Edwards spent over twenty years as a medical research scientist and chief of the division of infectious diseases, Harbor UCLA Medical Center developing a vaccine for severe candida infections, a form of yeast infection. His dream was to have his drug tested and eventually used in human patients. At this writing, a vaccine against recurrent vulvovaginitis has completed a successful FDA Phase II clinical trial; Dr. Edwards has realized at least one of his dreams.

The Dream

Dr. Jack Edwards's vision started with a female patient who had a very serious eye infection, which turned out to be candida, a form of fungal infection. The candida organism had entered her blood stream and lodged in her eye, partially blinding her. At the time, infections by candida were becoming much more frequent due to advances in medical therapies. (Some of the medications that treat chronic medical conditions can weaken the immune system and increase the risk for yeast infections. Having a compromised immune system can make it more difficult to fight off infection.[8]) To develop a treatment, or prevention, for candida infections, Dr. Edwards investigated how candida adheres to human endothelial cells (the cells of the interior lining of blood vessels). He wanted to determine what the adherence mechanism is, and if there is a way to prevent adherence, thereby making it impossible for the organism to infect vital organs.

Dr. Edwards performed numerous experiments from 1972 to 2003, to determine how the organism attached to and invaded human cells. To develop the technology to perform these experiments, Dr. Edwards made many trips to the National Institutes of Health (NIH) to learn and develop the techniques. During this process, he also learned other important characteristics of endothelial cell physiology.

Today, there is a new field of molecular biology related to fungal infections of humans that did not exist when Dr. Edwards's work started. It is now possible to determine which genes in candida are responsible for producing cell surface proteins. By using a technique called surrogate genetics, Dr. Edwards and his colleagues identified a cell surface protein on candida responsible for its adherence to human cells, and they were able to produce it, by recombinant technology, in large enough quantities to determine if it could function as a vaccine in experimental animal models.

Why did he choose this path? The patient not only had a severe, perplexing problem, she also focused Dr. Edwards's attention on candida infections. After reading extensively about candida, Dr. Edwards realized that the patient's problem was an important signal for an increase in the number of patients with the related problem of hematogenously disseminated candidiasis. The organism lives normally in most humans as part of normal flora, and does not cause problems unless patients are treated with newer therapies and with certain medical devices that create concentration points in the human body for infection.

Those newer therapies include, but are not limited to, powerful, broad spectrum antibiotics, immunosuppressive therapy to prevent transplanted organ rejection, cancer treatment that impairs the immune system, and indwelling medical devices such as intravenous catheters. These are just a few examples of modern therapeutics that turn this normally noninvasive commensal (symbiotic with) organism into an organism having the potential to be fatal when it enters the blood stream and then is spread to various organs, such as the eye, but also the brain, heart, kidneys, and other important tissues. In other words, problems with this organism are a trade off for modern medical advances.

Now candida is the fourth most common organism obtained from blood in hospitalized patients, the most common organism infecting intravenous catheters, and there are thousands of cases of infection every year, especially in countries with advanced medical care. Even with treatment, approximately 40 percent of patients whose bloodstream is invaded by candida do not survive.

Help from Grant Funding

Dr. Edwards and his colleagues received two successive, competitive, five-year NIH grants to study the mechanics of adherence of candida organisms to human endothelial cells, and to answer the question, "Can the ALS-3 protein (the cell surface protein adhesin) work as a vaccine in mice?" Once they had the protein it would be easy to immunize mice and determine its effectiveness as a vaccine in this preclinical model.

At that time, more biotech research projects were being developed in startup companies, because the large pharmaceutical companies had decided that it takes too long to develop new products. They left the risky part to the startup companies, and, if they saw a product they liked in a startup company, they acquired either the product or the company.

In 2003 Dr. Edwards and his team realized they would not be able to get enough federal funding to complete the work they had begun on a candida vaccine in clinical trials. They decided they needed commercial (venture) capital. During that same year, Ken Trevett, the CEO of L.A. County Research Education Institute (Now Los Angeles Biomedical Research Institute), asked me to help Dr. Edwards commercialize his technology. When I first met Dr. Edwards, his group was busy testing the vaccine in mice with very encouraging results.

At this time, Dr. Edwards was consumed by managing the infectious diseases department of Los Angeles Bio-Medical Research Institute and the Harbor-UCLA Medical Center, participating in the Infectious Diseases Society of America Public Policy efforts, and making rounds at the Harbor-UCLA Medical Center. He was spread too thin to have time to manage a commercialization effort. Dr. Edwards said, "There was no time to read *How to Start a Company*. This was perfect timing, and I was glad to have a business partner. Without one, we would still be looking for grant funding."

Beginning the Commercialization Process

My first step in commercializing the vaccine, which involved the help of several class teams from USC's entrepreneurship program, was to perform market and competitive analysis on the vaccine. It quickly became clear that the market opportunity was very large, and there was little or no competition.

We formed NovaDigm Therapeutics, Inc. in 2006 as LA BioMed's commercial partner in a proposed federal Small Business Technology Transfer (STTR) grant. As the company progressed, we found that government grants made us more attractive to venture capitalists, and the prospect of raising venture capital made us more attractive to the grant agencies—an extremely positive feedback loop.

In 2007 we approached several venture capital firms and in 2008 we received an $18 million commitment from Domain Associates, one of the top biotech venture capital firms in the United States. Once the first tranche of the investment was in the bank, I orchestrated an effort to recruit an experienced vaccine-industry CEO, which led us to Dr. Timothy Cooke. Dr. Cooke started as NovaDigm's CEO in 2009 and remains in that position at this writing.

NovaDigm's initial business concept was to create what we called "another Amgen," a company with the ability to develop multiple fungal vaccines and take them to market. We quickly learned that, while this kind of portfolio approach might work for a public company, Domain wanted to fund one vaccine and then find a buyer for either the drug or the company. At a time when the IPO market was robust, we might have been able to pursue the drug portfolio approach, but the IPO market almost completely closed down when the dot-com bubble burst, and it had yet not recovered in 2008.

But the drug-resistance problem had become even more serious; there was now a huge problem with hospital-acquired infections. Vaccines are a better solution than antibiotics, because there is less opportunity for fungi or bacteria to learn resistance. At this writing, NovaDigm Therapeutics recently completed a Phase II clinical trial for the use of the vaccine to protect patients against an infection called recurrent candida vulvovaginitis. The company has at least two other vaccines poised for clinical trials.

Over the past seven years, NovaDigm's vision has continued to evolve. It has acquired additional antigens, and it has discovered other closely related infectious diseases that it can treat. NovaDigm has not become a full portfolio company, but it has become an engine for the creation of certain fungal and bacterial vaccines, including vaccines to protect against recurring vulvovaginitis, acinetobacter, and cystic fibrosis.

Dr. Edwards says, "Of course, I'm willing to take business advice; that's a no-brainer. I learn something every day. There's enormous value in having experience, whether it's in medicine or business. It has been interesting to learn about a field in which I have no experience [business). I have also enjoyed the ongoing relationships with Nova-Digm's CEO, Tim Cooke, John Hennessey, the chief scientific officer, the directors, the investors, and all members of the team. It's all been extremely stimulating and gratifying."

(My interview with Dr. Jack Edwards, Founder of NovaDigm Therapeutics, Inc. was held on November 3, 2015.)

Conclusion

A startup company's best chance of attracting capital is to create as much value as possible before approaching investors. A company's stock can be used to build a fledgling team of people capable of developing a prototype, building a product, obtaining customers, or taking other steps that add value to the startup. This process shows investors that the startup company's leaders are competent, it separates the startup from competition, and it increases the company's valuation.

In the next and final chapter, we will summarize our views about this most critical aspect of creating a successful startup company—leadership. We have come full circle back to the question of who is the best leader for a startup company. You won't be surprised at the answer, but let's complete the logic and explore the considerations in chapter 13: "Follow the Leader."

CHAPTER 13

Follow the Leader

Alice said, "Would you tell me, please,
which way I ought to go from here?"
"That depends a good deal on where
you want to get to," said the Cat.
"I don't much care where—" said Alice.
"Then it doesn't matter which way you go," said the Cat.

—Lewis Carroll, *Alice's Adventures in Wonderland*

In this chapter, we will synthesize our concepts of leadership. What kind of leadership is required to build a successful startup? Where do leadership skills come from? How do startups assemble the leadership skills required for success?

We will learn from the experience of Josh Roach, founder of Boost Academy, Inc.

Focus on Leadership

We started this book by celebrating a few entrepreneurs who led their companies through multiple growth phases to spectacular success. However, the ability to do this is extremely rare. In the early 1980s, only one California company with revenues in excess of $100 million was still managed by its founder: California Microwave, Inc. was still managed by its founder, David Leeson.. Since then, we have witnessed the successes of Steve Jobs, Bill Gates, Mark Zuckerberg, and a few others, but these exceptions validate the rule that experienced CEOs and company builders make the best leaders, contrary to what Steve Jobs Law claims—that founders make the best leaders.

Leadership is a combination of clear vision, accurate assessment of opportunities, and knowing what to do next in order to fulfill the vision. Creating a successful startup company is a challenging task. First-time CEOs rarely have the insight to properly analyze a company's situation and conceive and implement an effective strategy.

Assembling Skills

One of the challenges of company building is to keep realistic expectations with respect to the ever-changing demands of the CEO position. Founders have a tendency to underestimate the challenges, which is responsible for many high-tech failures.

Rather than immediately trying to raise capital, a founder with a blockbuster idea would be better served to create a founding team that can create some initial value and then seek an experienced leader for his company. This leader will develop an effective strategy and have a much better chance of attracting capital and building a successful business.

As we have seen, the leader of a high-tech startup is confronted with a daunting collection of chicken and egg problems. It's difficult to hire staff without capital, and it's difficult to get capital without staff. It's difficult to create a product without staff, and it's difficult to attract staff without a product. It's difficult to find a good CEO without capital, and it's difficult to get capital without a top CEO.

Each of these challenges can be overcome by a gradual, step-by-step sequence of small steps. Creative leaders offer stock options to founders in order to build a small team. If the product isn't too complicated, this virtual staff can develop a first version of the product. With a virtual team and a working product in place, a company has a reasonable chance of attracting a small amount of capital and/or an experienced CEO, either of which creates more value.

This strategy of adding value in small steps is the secret to building many high-tech companies. It requires a powerful combination of strategic thinking, vision, and patience. It is entirely consistent with our recommended strategy for bootstrapping value when possible. Building team, building product, creating customers, attracting management, and attracting capital are all value-creating steps and critical stepping stones on the pathway to success

Leadership of the Fundable Startup

The best leaders have a realistic view of their own strengths and weaknesses. They assemble a team with all of the skills that will be required for success. They also make sure that the members of the team have skills that complement any weaknesses the founder may have.

A founder must answer the question "do I have the management skills to build this company?" And "do I have the skills that will make me a fundable CEO in the eyes of venture capitalists?" Answering these questions honestly and accurately requires extraordinary clear-headed self-assessment. The answers to these questions can make or break a startup company. If a founder who in truth is not qualified to be a fundable CEO can see herself as venture capitalists will see her, she may be motivated to find the right kind of CEO partner instead.

CASE STUDY

Josh Roach, founder of Boost Academy, Builds a Bridge to Finding a CEO

Josh Roach has been through two IPOs. He is a very seasoned and hands-on technology manager, and several times he has managed an organization of up to two hundred people. He works hard to keep current with the technologies related to his company. Josh believes that keeping up with technology is one of his keys to survival.

Josh is an experienced technology manager, yet he chose to follow a bootstrap approach to building his new company, Boost Academy. Boost Academy, has "happy, paying customers," which is a very good place to start.

The Beginnings

From 2008 to 2012, Josh was an employee at Mitek Systems, Inc., a mobile imaging company, whose patented document capture software allows a consumer to use the camera on a smartphone or tablet to take a photo of a document in order to deposit a check or pay a bill. Mitek's unique solutions enable organizations across industries to differentiate themselves from their competitors, attract and retain customers, and ultimately increase their revenue and profitability.

Mitek had some problems. They had just been delisted from the NASDAQ when Josh joined the company to help turn it around. The company had an OCR (optical character recognition) device which could scan 3-D color-graphic information into a smartphone. This enabled a variety of mobile applications. Three years later, Josh and other members of his team rang the NASDAQ closing bell on behalf of Mitek. Their effort to rescue Mitek had been a great success. For Josh, this was a real eye-opener. He learned a lot about mobile technology, and he saw the value of connecting a mobile device to the cloud.

Working with four Russian PhD scientists, Josh showed Bank of America that he could take a picture of a check with the same accuracy as an ATM scan. Bank of America bought the idea, as did Chase Bank, Citibank, and Wells Fargo. Josh was excited by the ability to deposit a check by scanning it on a smartphone. He spent four years at Mitek working on this problem. Smartphone scanning is a powerful alternative to handing a check to a bank teller or depositing it into an ATM.

After leaving Mitek, Josh decided to develop a live collaboration on mobile computing using an iPad. He felt that the format could be very exciting. He conceptualized an iPad-to-iPad remote system that would allow tutors to interact with their students. Josh's wife, Beth, had been director of product implementation for Computer Associates, Inc. (CAI), so she knew about various technologies. He discussed his idea with her, and because his wife liked the idea, Josh left Mitek to pursue it. Next, Josh recruited a number of tutors in exchange for one-half cash and one-half stock to test his concept.

Planning a Startup

Josh wrote a forty-page paper describing his remote tutoring system in which both the student and the tutor would use an iPad. He applied for four patents, which are currently pending.

Next, Josh approached four individuals he had worked with in the past, and he offered each of them a small percentage of equity (stock ownership) in the company if they would work with him for a year to develop the concept. The year turned out to be two and a half years, but the four colleagues are still working with Josh on the development of the tutoring system.

The team did not try to develop a prototype. They went directly to a strong product, the first in the industry. This initial product contained almost 100 percent of the features Josh envisioned for the finished tutoring system.

During this design and development process, Josh consulted with a number of high school math tutors who provided extremely useful advice. For example, he was planning to incorporate a "push to talk" feature that would allow either the tutor or the student to touch a soft "TALK" key on the iPad in order to initiate a two-way conversation. But the tutors felt that that would be too clumsy. Instead, they wanted to add a "voice over IP" (VOIP) conversation mode. VOIP is a communication protocol that enables telephone calls to be transmitted over the internet.

The tutors also came up with a concept of zooming-in to let the tutor draw or write on the document using a finger. When the tutor and the student zoom-out, the drawing or writing looks like an image created by a fine-point pen.

During the development cycle, Josh consulted ten tutors and asked them to provide various samples of math problems that would come up in tutoring sessions, such as quadratic equations. Through this process, he assembled over 6,000 worksheets, which can be referenced by the student independently.

Another important design concept is the notion of playback, which permits the student to replay selected portions of a tutoring session, like a video recording, in case she needs help in remembering what was said during the tutoring session.

At the end of a tutoring session, the student's parent receives a short summary of the session by email. The tutor might want to notify the parent, for example, that he assigned some exercises to the student. This notification lets parents essentially look over their child's shoulder during the tutoring process.

Bootstrapping (Almost)

The startup process for Boost Academy has not been entirely cash-free. Because of his earlier business successes, Josh was in the fortunate position of being able to provide about $150,000, with help from his friends. He's been able, fortunately, to work for two years without a real salary.

The Bridge to Finding a CEO

Based on their initial product development and marketing success, the team raised $350,000 in angel capital during 2013 and 2014. The company attracted the attention of Craig Collins, who had been CEO of Perinova and a cofounder and vice president of marketing of Supply-Pro. After extensive due diligence, Craig decided to invest in the company, and he helped put together a $650,000 investment round. As part of his due diligence process, Craig interviewed some of the tutors. Referring to Josh, one said to Craig, "This guy will put me out of business." That seemed to Craig to be an excellent endorsement of Josh's ideas.

Josh did not want to hire a CEO until he had a working product. But as this round of financing came together, and Craig became more involved, it made sense to install Craig as CEO. So far, the company is populated only by engineers, tutors, Craig, as CEO, and a VP of marketing. Craig recruited a full-time tutor administrator, who now has over twenty tutors. All of the tutors are highly rated. Most have graduate degrees.

The tutors have provided a lot of extremely useful feedback during the development process. The system has been designed to simulate a one-on-one tutoring session. The designers tried to imagine a perfect tutoring session being filmed, so that it could be reviewed afterward. Then they built a system to create the same kind of experience.

All of the developers have a strong background in mathematics, algorithm development, and engineering. They understand how to manage the modeling and logical processes that Boost's software must provide.

Technically, the company was almost insolvent; it did not have enough cash to pay its bills, but Craig helped to raise $925,000, some of which has come from parents of students, which is an extremely compelling endorsement of the Boost concept.

Josh and Craig want to complete a $500,000 round now. $100,000 is committed, so they still need to raise $400,000. They are expecting to retain a finder to help raise the next round of $5 million.

One of Josh's lessons learned is that online advertising for tutors has been very effective.

At this writing, Craig is acting as the primary sales professional for the company. The other staff refer to Craig as the parent whisperer, because he communicates so effectively with the parents of the students, who, of course, are the real customers.

Boost's competition is Mathnasium, Sylvan Learning, and Kumon. Boost's primary competitive advantage over these firms is the power of its online, iPad-based platform.

Revenues are growing rapidly. In August 2014, there were thirteen paid sessions. In April 2015, there were 350 sessions. The money that the company is raising now will be used to triple the company's marketing resources. They plan to offer salesmen a $50,000 base salary plus commissions.

Boost Academy is a sort of Uber for tutors. It facilitates quick and easy matching. The tutor presses "now" to accept a new student, which is similar to a Uber driver being the first to respond to a dispatch call for a passenger.

The company gives the first lesson for free. So far, 98 percent of its free first lessons have converted to paying customers.

Each tutor has two subjects, or types of classes, right now, and focuses on two to three grade levels.

Craig has the marketing activity revved up and ready to go. The $500,000 should permit a tripling or quadrupling of the company's number of paid sessions and revenues.

Boost Academy met several of its investors through Monday Club, even though Monday Club is not primarily an investment source. However, it is a good network of company builders, and it often provides a path to capital for its presenters.

Now that Boost Academy has happy paying customers, it needs additional funds to expand its marketing activities. The company intends to use market analytics to determine the best pay-per-view and other social media marketing strategies.

Josh recalls, "Mark Twain said, 'I wouldn't want to be a member of a club that would have me as a member.'" In the same spirit, Josh says, "If I wouldn't invest in me as the CEO, then why would anyone else? Fortunately, Craig Collins is not a big-company kind of guy. I don't want a big-company executive to come in and try to build a large administrative staff. We need to stay lean."

(From my interview with Josh Roach,
Founder of Boost Academy, Inc. on December 14, 2015.)

The key to a successful bootstrap, according to Josh, is to "roll up your sleeves and prove to your team that you can get in the trenches." But once the company is launched, you turn your attention to expansion and growth.

Follow the Leader

> 66 The best CEOs I know are teachers,
> and at the core of what they teach is strategy. 99
>
> —Michael Porter, *Strategy Bites Back*

In order to move a company from startup to $100 million in sales, a leader must have enormous capacity to grow as her company passes through the phases of one level of management, and then two levels, and then three or more. Listed below are some management structures that require very different kinds of leadership skills:

1. Managing a startup when only a few technical people are involved.

2. Managing a startup with a flat management structure, meaning that almost all employees report to the CEO.

3. Managing C level executives; that is, executives who manage other people. This requires much more senior-level management experience than managing a flat organization.

4. Managing an organization that has more than three levels of boxes on an organizational chart. As an organization grows to this structure and beyond, the CEO must have excellent leadership and communication skills.

The demands on a leader never stop growing. Even if the founder manages to launch her company and raise initial capital, she is likely to be severely challenged by the requirements imposed by subsequent expansion and growth. The wise founder or board of directors knows when and how to get help.

Conclusion

Are great leaders born, or are they made? In the high-tech world, there have been a few natural leaders who seemed to have an innate sense of what to do at each step—and the skills required to build a company. But, as we saw in chapter 8, the skills required of a fundable CEO are extensive, mostly unintuitive, and difficult to learn. The successful founder or CEO is indeed a rare person! Imagine how many more startups could be successful if the founder simply made a clear-headed self-assessment and took the steps needed to recruit a capable management team and CEO in order to create a fundable and successful startup.

Famous football player, coach, and executive Vince Lombardi said it well:

> " Contrary to the opinion of many, leaders are not born; they are made. And they are made by hard effort, which is the price we must all pay for success. "
>
> —Vince Lombardi, *What It Takes to Be #1*

Endnotes

Chapter One

1. "Steve Jobs's Law: Why Founders Make the Best Leaders," James Kwak, TheAtlantic.com, September 1, 2011.

Chapter Two

1. Ian Hathaway, "Tech Starts: High-Technology Business Formation and Job Creation in the United States," Kaufman Foundation Research Reports, August 2013, accessed September 11, 2015. http://www.kauffman.org/~/media/kauffman_org/research%20 reports%20and%20covers/2013/08/bdstechstartsreport.pdf

2. Brad Sugars, "How Many Jobs CanYour Startup Create this Year?" Entrepreneur.com, January 11, 2012, accessed January 2, 2017. https://www.entrepreneur.com/article/222568

3. "Frequently Asked Questions about Small Business," SBA Office of Advocacy, September, 2012, accessed January 2, 2017. www.sba.gov/advocacy

4. Rebecca O. Bagley, "Small Business = Big Impact," forbes.com, May 15, 2012, accessed July 18, 2015. http://www.forbes.com/sites/rebeccabagley/2012/05/15/small-businesses -big-impact/

5. "Technology and Our Economy," Microsoft, On the Issues: Society and Technology, September 30, 1999, accessed June 26, 2015. http://www.microsoft.com/issues/essays/1999/09-20tech.mspx

6. "Technical Progress Function," Investopedia, accessed January 2, 2017. http://www.investopedia.com/terms/t/technical-progress-function.asp

7. Enrique Martinez-Garcia, "Technological Progress Is Key to Improving World Living Standards," Federal Reserve Bank of Dallas, Economic Letter index, Vol. 8, No. 4, June 2013, accessed January 2, 2017. https://www.dallasfed.org/research/eclett/2013/el1304.cfm

8. Julie Bick, "The Microsoft Millionaires Come of Age," *New York Times*, May 29, 2005, accessed January 4, 2017.
http://www.nytimes.com/2005/05/29/business/yourmoney/the-microsoft -millionaires-come-of-age.html?_r=1.

9. Daniel Eran Dilger, "Apple, Inc. stock IPO created 300 millionaires 33 years ago today," December 12, 2013, Appleinsider, accessed January 4, 2017.
http://appleinsider.com/articles/13/12/12/apple-inc-stock-ipo-created- 300-millionaires-33-years-ago-today.

Chapter Three

1. David S. Rose, quora.com. "Is It Possible for an Idea to Be Funded by a VC?," November 12, 2012, accessed on September 11, 2015.
http://www.quora.com/Is-it-possible-for-an-idea-to-be-funded-by-a-VC.

2. Max Marmer et. al, "A Deep Dive Into Why Most High Growth Startups Fail," Startup Genome Report Extra, March 2012, accessed on February 18, 2017.
http://gallery.mailchimp.com/8c534f3b5ad611c0ff8aeccd5/files/Startup_ Genome_Report_Extra_Premature_Scaling_version_2.1.pdfs.

3. "Startup Business Failure Rate by Industry," statisticbrain.com. February 5, 2015, accessed on July 16, 2015.
http://www.statisticbrain.com/startup-failure-by-industry/.

4. Patricia Schaefer, "The Seven Pitfalls of Business Failure and How to Avoid Them," accessed on July 16, 2015.
http://www.businessknowhow.com/startup/business-failure.htm

5. Deborah Gage, "The Venture Capital Secret: 3 Out of 4 Start-ups Fail," wsj.com, September 20, 2012, accessed July 19, 2015.
http://www.wsj.com/articles/SB10000872396390443720204578004980476429190.

Chapter Four

1. Charles Francis Drexel was a mechanical engineer, researcher, and Inventor.
http://www.colorado.edu/engineering/deaa/cgi-bin/display.pl?id=172 Website accessed on June 8, 2017.

Chapter Five

1. Professor Jay Ritter, "Historical U.S. IPO Statistics," quandl.com, accessed on April 16, 2016. https://www.quandl.com/data/RITTER/US_IPO_STATS-Historical -US-IPO-Statistics.

2. David Gleba, "VC Winners of 1992," *Upside* magazine, February, 1993.

3. "The IPO Buzz: Road to Recovery," IPOScoop.com, March 22, 2009, accessed October 21, 2015. http://www.iposcoop.com/the-ipo-buzz-road-to-recovery/.

4. Xiaohui Gao et al., "Where Have All the IPOs Gone?" SEC Advisory Committee on Small and Emerging Companies, September 2012, accessed January 3, 2017. https://www.sec.gov/info/smallbus/acsec/acsec-090712-ritter-slides.pdf

5. Erin Griffith, "This Chart Shows the Future of Venture Capital," Pando, accessed on February 17, 2017. https://pando.com/2013/08/28/this-chart-shows-the-future-of-venture-capital/

6. "U.S. Money Tree Report," PWC, The Money Tree, accessed January 2, 2017. https://www.pwcmoneytree.com/HistoricTrends/ CustomQueryHistoricTrend

7. "Our Mission is to Help Bring Creative Projects to Life," accessed February 17, 2017. https://www.kickstarter.com/about?ref=nav

Chapter Six

1. Quoted in Carol J. Loomis, *Tap Dancing to Work: Warren Buffett on Practically Everything, 1966-2013*, (New York: Portfolio; Reprint Edition, 2013)

2. George Garza, edited by Lamar Stonecypher, "The History of Cisco," Brighthub.com, updated: 1/9/2011.

3. The network, Cisco's Technology news website, accessed April 17, 2016. https://newsroom.cisco.com/execbio-detail?articleId=33773

Chapter Seven

1. "Methicillin-resistant *Staphylococcus aureus* (MRSA)," Centers for Disease Control, accessed February 10, 2017. https://www.cdc.gov/mrsa/tracking/

2. "Invasive Candidiasis Statistics," Centers for Disease Control, accessed February 10, 2017. https://www.cdc.gov/fungal/diseases/candidiasis/invasive/statistics.html

Chapter Eight

1. Michael Porter, *Competitive Strategy: Techniques for Analyzing Industries and Competitors*, 1980 (New York: The Free Press, a Division of Simon & Schuster).

2. "DRC Computer Establishes Stunning Genomics World Record," pharmiweb.com, accessed September 25, 2015. http://www.pharmiweb.com/pressreleases/pressrel.asp?ROW_ID =35039#.VgXmx85xY7B

3. "Intel's $16.7 Billion Altera Deal Is Fueled by Data Centers," bloomberg.com, accessed on October 21, 2015. http://www.bloomberg.com/news/articles/2015-06-01/intel-buys -altera-for-16-7-billion-as-chip-deals-accelerate.

Chapter Nine

1. "Want to Be a CEO? Stay Put," forbes.com, accessed September 25, 2015. http://www.forbes.com/2003/03/31/cx_wt_0401exec.html

2. "2015 CEO Transitions," spencerstuart.com, accessed on February 19, 2017. https://www.spencerstuart.com/research-and-insight/2015-ceo -transitions.

Chapter Ten

1. Richard A. Riley, "Paying Unregistered Finders to Raise Capital for Your Company is Generally Illegal," Hawley Troxell, accessed April 17, 2016. http://archive.constantcontact.com/fs020/1102520666121/ archive/1103181251986.html

2. "How Do You Become a Chef and How Long Does It Take?" International Culinary Center, accessed June 8, 2016. http://www.internationalculinarycenter.com/culinary-topics/how-long -does-it-take-to-become-a-chef.

Chapter Eleven

1. Scott A. Shane, *Fool's Gold?: The Truth Behind Angel Investing in America* (New York: Oxford University Press, 2009. p. 14.

Chapter Twelve

1. "Number of Jobs Held, Labor Market Activity, and Earnings Growth Among the Youngest Baby Boomers: Results from a Longitudinal Survey," Bureau of Labor Statistics, accessed February 21, 2017. https://www.bls.gov/news.release/archives/nlsoy_09102010.pdf.

2. Blaise Pascal, *Provincial Letters*: Letter XVI (4 December 1656).

3. "Hatching Ideas, and Companies, by the Dozens at M.I.T., Hannah Seligson, *New York Times*, accessed January 6, 2017. www.nytimes.com.

4. Koch Institute for Integrative Cancer Research at MIT, Massachusetts Institute of Technology, The Langer Lab, accessed May 21, 2017. http://langer-lab.mit.edu/research.

5. "Building New Life Sciences Companies: The Bob Langer-Terry McGuire Show on Video," accessed on January 6, 2017, Wade Roush. www.xconomy.com, October 22, 2008.

6. Polaris Partners, accessed January 7, 2017, http://www.polarispartners.com/polaris-team/.

7. "Scientist Gives VC an Edge," Rebecca Buckman, *The Wall Street Journal*, Updated April 14, 2008, accessed January 6, 2017. www.wsj.com.

8. Mary Elizabeth Dallas, "Conditions that Increase your Risk for Yeast Infections," Everyday Health, accessed February 23, 2017. http://www.everydayhealth.com/hs/understanding-yeast-infection/ conditions-that-increase-your-risk-for-yeast-infection/

Index

About the Author

Photo by David Fairchild Studio (http://davidfairchildstudio.com)

Fred M. Haney, PhD, has been actively involved in the creation of high-tech businesses from six different perspectives: as cofounder and chairman of four startups, active director of over twenty companies, and as mentor, angel investor, venture capital fund manager, and corporate strategic-planning executive.

Dr. Haney served as the founding chairman of NovaDigm Therapeutics, DRC, Inc., Media Matchmaker, Inc., and PulSentry, Inc. At NovaDigm and DRC, he managed strategies that led to the "Series A" infusion of over $25 Million in venture capital, and he recruited experienced CEOs to manage the further growth and success of the companies.

Dr. Haney has been a hands-on director of over twenty high-tech startup companies, four of which were public companies, including Rainbow Technologies, Inc. (Nasdaq: RNBO).

In 1984 Dr. Haney founded Monday Club, which has grown into a mentoring network of 850 members that operates in Santa Monica, Torrance, and Orange County, California. Monday Club has helped over 400 companies improve their business plans, raise capital, and find key advisors and directors.

In 1997 Dr. Haney was one of ten cofounders of Tech Coast Angels, one of the largest angel investment groups in the United States.

Dr. Haney was the founder and manager of 3i Ventures, California, a subsidiary of London's 3i Group plc, the world's largest venture capital company. He managed the successful investment of $60 Million in eighty startup companies producing nineteen IPOs and twenty acquisitions.

Early in his career, Dr. Haney managed strategic planning organizations for Xerox Corp., Computer Sciences Corporation Infonet Division and TRW, Inc. At TRW, he facilitated the sale of the TRW Datacom International Division, and he managed the turnaround and sale of the TRW Vidar Transmission Products Division.

Dr. Haney published *My Doggie Says . . . Messages from Jamie*, an award-winning book of stories about how his golden retriever communicated various "messages" through her behavior. The book's "messages" are illustrated by eighty-five color photographs.

Dr. Haney received a PhD degree in Computer Science from Carnegie-Mellon University, an MS in Mathematics from Colorado State University, and a BA in Mathematics from Ohio Wesleyan University.